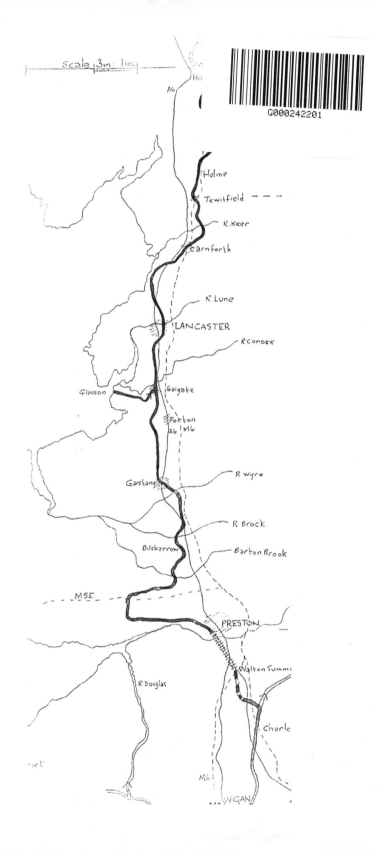

scale 3m: 1ins

Holme
Tewitfield
R. Keer
Carnforth
R. Lune
LANCASTER
R CONDER
Glasson
Galgate
Forton
A6 M6
R Wyre
Garstang
R Brock
Bilsborrow
Barton Brook
M55
PRESTON
Walton Summit
R. Douglas
Chorley
M61
WIGAN

As If...

"This is such a creative idea for a book. The approach, Gill's life experience, and how she uses it all to tell this story, to minister, and to fascinate is just excellent. 'As If - Steering your Life without Strife, Navigating from Fantasy to Faith and rising from Delusion into Destiny' is a truly wonderful book"

Markus McDowell - author & editor,
https://markusmcdowell.com

"Every destination has a journey and every promise has a process. Too often we hijack our destiny by trying to take the shortcut; cut out the journey, cut out the process, cut out the stress, cut out the challenges or perhaps cut out the obstacles. But 'what if' we lived 'as if' who we're becoming is more important than where we're going? Maybe our commitment to the process would solidify our determination to get to the promise? Maybe our experiences would determine our expectations?

Follow this inspiring journey with Gill through her interpretation of the valley of the shadow of death. That is, through the obstacles and every other barrier that you thought disarmed your destiny, when in fact they'd empowered it. There's a towering flight of locks in front of you - and the views are spectacular"

Matt Boyle - Doncaster Campus Pastor,
Legacy Church UK

"Your book speaks to me of reassurance of my calling, that it's already written and now I must learn to live it. The creative approach taken, plaiting together three perspectives throughout the book powerfully express Gill's intended message of navigating life's complexity.

As an outdoor painter I find the colourful narrative and imagery of life on a canal boat breathtaking. Gill's vulnerability is honest and relatable. This has been a refreshing experience for me spiritually and intellectually. 'As If' is a totally inspiring read for me, as a Christian and as a reflective observer of people".

Andrew Farmer - Associate Member of
The Royal Institute of Oil Painters

"The image of Forton, a small Lancastrian village where major roads, canal and railway meet, is a perfect one to summarise 'As If'. Life converges on us all; the good, the bad and the ugly. We often want to speed through the difficulties as if on the M6, or revel in the joys - steadily on a narrow boat. Life doesn't always work like that, but if we can understand Gill's leading that we live in the reality of accomplished dreams, of completed work, and of fulfilled hope, then the joys of life are deepened and the pain placed into a proper context."

"'As If' is an emotive, personal and powerful exploration of journeys past, present and future that will help you discover that dreams and destiny are never truly lost if you choose the right 'As If'; living 'As If' they have already come to pass rather than 'As If' they never will. This book reaches to the high-flyers and the down-in-the-doldrums, and challenges all of us to allow ourselves to redefine our past to shape our future".

Robert Ridler - Teacher and Lecturer
Legacy Church, MA (Th)

"Twenty years of thought, the wisdom born of hindsight, along with vision for the future, have been the foundation of Gill Bentham's latest book, a kind of prequel to her first, 'Disentangling Genius'.... I look forward to the impact of Gill's 'water borne Pilgrim's Progress for the 21st century'. I similarly desire to see the generational impact of these deep truths and the rising generation being able to learn from struggles and mistakes that we have made (including Gill, who has made herself vulnerable in her writing).

I want to see the new Pilgrim rise up, but one who is dead to himself, is a laid down warrior lover and will do whatever it takes as dead man for the kingdom. One who is equipped with keys to open locks such as Gill supplies in 'As If'"

Lisa Miara - Founder/President
USA Springs of Hope Foundation Inc
Springs of Hope Foundation, Iraq

"Having known Gill for many years now, I know her book 'As If', is written from her learnt experiences and love for communicating with others. I am sure this book will be a blessing and help to many people"

Grayson Jones – Senior Leader, Legacy Network

"'As If', is a fine example of a testimonial, an exemplar of a dedicated Christian's journey. Gill has a good command of the writer's craft. The work, using the canal theme, to carry her spiritual message, is a convincing device. She described the book as a pilgrim's progress. It reads as such…an account of the Christian awakening. Her fount of knowledge of the Bible and her interpretative understanding of its Scriptures make 'As If' a challenging and rewarding read. With admiration"

Dad - (Bentley, Edward Shaw 23rd November 2016)

AS IF

Steering your Life without Strife, Navigating from Fantasy to Faith and Rising from Delusion into Destiny

I pray great blessing
and breakthrough after
breakthrough on your life
and Springs of Hope Foundation.
Brave warrior, Lisa!

Love Gill x   June 2019.

GILL BENTHAM

Author Academy Elite
As If. Steering your Life without Strife, Navigating from Fantasy to Faith and Rising from Delusion into Destiny
Copyright © 2019 by Gill Bentham
This title is also available as an Author Academy Elite ebook
This title is also available as an Audible edition

Paperback: 978-1-946114-93-8
Hardback: 978-1-64085-024-8
Ebook: 978-1-64085-025-5
Library of Congress Control Number: 2017908001

For my unborn great-grand-daughter.

And, importantly for my late Dad who read this unpublished draft in the last months of life as an agnostic. You infused me with love and appreciation for the countryside, for beauty, art and form, a fascination with words, ideas and communication, a sensitivity of soul and an eternal search for meaning and significance. You found hope and vision in the metaphor of *As If* and through it, received back the gift of faith - after all the years of investment in my capacity to learn and to inspire.

Thank you.

"Your eyes saw my unformed substance and in Your book all the days [of my life] were written before ever they took shape, when as yet there was none of them"

Psalm 139:16

CONTENTS

FOREWORD

Gill's first book, *Disentangling Genius*, was a bold, arresting statement of passion for purposeful living.

Now, I'm excited to reveal what seems to be its prequel: *As If: Steering your Life without Strife, Navigating from Fantasy to Faith and rising from Delusion into Destiny. As If* puts *Disentangling Genius* firmly into context and explains the first volume's particularly raw and colourful explosion.

This time, Gill dives into a fresh metaphor of the British waterway. Powerfully imaginative scenes of this neglected mode of transport are described with nostalgic affection. Utilizing carefully crafted vignettes, she interrupts these scenes. These are commentaries from her future self as an 89-year-old grandmother on a day trip with her great-granddaughter. She views her life from completion—as if it has all unfolded.

Throughout, Gill compares her life with that of Jacob, the dubious Bible character (famed for impatience and striving). Presenting powerfully descriptive imagery of the lazily stagnant canal waterway, Gill navigates readers into the call for yet deeper levels of intimacy with God rather than attaining to a higher state of perfection or performance.

Gill tells me this concept was 'downloaded' in one moment— twenty years ago. However, I can see why it needed to emerge in its own timeframe, having been gently infusing since it inspired her attention.

Despite the detail and intricacy of this multi-layered and emotive work, Gill's use of metaphor is simple and enduring. She may just have opened a new niche—that of the sophisticated and acutely observant inspirational. Using evocative language and honest soul searching, Gill handles an incredible number of layers and themes, authentically reflecting and plumbing the depth of your soul with hers.

In her imaginary and prophetically visual metaphorical style, Gill provides a running commentary on the stretching and growing experience of the Christian soul as deep calls to deep. Yes, still waters really do run deep, and Gill is an example of this, both in person and in her art.

Kary Oberbrunner — *Author of ELIXIR Project, Day Job to Dream Job, The Deeper Path, and Your Secret Name*

PREFACE

What do you want to be?

When adults ask children about their aspirations, they don't say, *"Who do you think you are?"* They say, *"What do you want to be?"*

It's a simple as that with God. He knows who you are and will never cast doubt upon that. Everything you want to be is in the bulls-eye of His will. You can expect Him to return it to you as you seek it. I will keep mentioning this fact - *it* returns! This means it comes back. It returns because it has been with you once before.

'When did I have this before?' you might ask.

And I merely require you to consider this fact. There is a book of words already written about you. In fact, it pre-existed you; before you even breathed, believed or disbelieved this fact.

It just is. Your purpose has already been written.

"All the days ordained for me were written in your book before one of them came to be"

(Psalm 139:16, NIV)

"This grace was given us in Christ Jesus before the beginning of time"

(2 Timothy 1:9b, NIV)

It says who you are and what you will be.
To set it free, it needs to be believed and declared.
Only once you are co-operating with Him in the pursuit of its return will it be fulfilled. Sometimes you will encounter seemingly impassable obstructions. Like the solid lock gates in the waterway of a canal cruise you have planned.
You are supposed to claim the return of each word that is caught in a seemingly impassable lock, and that might take some conservation work of His original course or plan.

"Prepare for GOD's arrival!
Make the road straight and smooth,
a highway fit for our God.
Fill in the valleys,
level off the hills,
Smooth out the ruts,
clear out the rocks.
Then GOD's bright glory will shine
and everyone will see it.
Yes. Just as GOD has said."

(Isaiah 40:3-5, The Message)

"And a highway will be there; it will be called the Way of Holiness. The unclean will not journey on it; it will be for those who walk in that Way; wicked fools will not go about on it."

(Isaiah 35:8, NIV)

Your call is to apply the knowledge of word keys, the windlass and opening mechanisms to the obstructive walls of the lock gates. Then they slowly swing, and you pass into the next open stretch of water, called the pound. Perhaps one or two smaller vessels can also pass with you, on the uplift of water that takes you and them out of confinement. People who pass that way can journey their way through to the One Way. That High waterway stretches on, far ahead of you. You and they are directed to it through faith and perseverance.

Something better lies ahead once you realise you have already been there.

> *"The path of right-living people is level.*
> *The Leveler evens the road for the right-living.*
> *We're in no hurry, GOD. We're content to linger*
> *in the path sign-posted with your decisions.*
> *Who you are and what you've done*
> *are all we'll ever want"*

(Isaiah 26:7-8, The Message)

"[Prompted] by faith Jacob, when he was dying, blessed each of Joseph's sons and bowed in prayer over the top of his staff"

(Hebrews 11:21)

"Then [Jacob] blessed Joseph and said God [Himself] before Whom my fathers Abraham and Isaac lived and walked habitually, God [Himself] Who has [been my Shepherd and has led and] fed me from the time I came into being until this day, The redeeming Angel [that is, the Angel the Redeemer-not a created being but the Lord Himself] Who has redeemed me continually from every evil, bless the lads! And let my name be perpetuated in them [may they be worthy of having their names coupled with mine], and the names of my fathers Abraham and Isaac; and let them become a multitude in the midst of the earth."

(Genesis 48:15-16)

INTRODUCTION

I'm Still Standing

The beginning of the book will have Trea, my seven-year-old great-granddaughter ask me "What are you?"

She is in complete ignorance of the enormity of this simple question. Am I a product of what I did? Who I knew? Where I went? What I desired?

I cast my mind back to the flurry of inspiration that was the time when I wrote my first book '*Disentangling Genius*'[1]. The start of my life as an author had been cathartic, an exciting and interactive process. Maybe this book will be my last? A bookend of the first?

Yes, I had always been a writer and had known this all along. So, *what* am I?

I am a testament to faith. I am a declaration of the timeless continuity of faith in the love of God for one ordinary life. Jacob's life, my life, Trea's life or your life! I am a declaration of His love for one family, one people, one nation, and one eternal Kingdom.

Disentangling Genius

Three main strands were described in the tale, in which I took stock of my formerly, frantically frustrated life.

A black, nightmare strand of fear had almost wrecked my sanity. Eventually, it redeemed itself as strength, clarity and a just return of all the desserts of my perseverance.

Then there was the red strand of self-conscious embarrassment that I finally re-interpreted as blood-red boldness and daring. Thirdly, I unpicked the bright green of demanding and overwhelming responsibility.

By my mid-forties, this tangled trio of colours had matted and caught on the spinning wheel of my life, and I had to cut loose, pay attention to the series of knots, gently coax, lean into and loosen the snags. The rest of my life had been a faithful and more selective design of these threads. Oh, and the green thread...it became the soft green element of recreation and playfulness. Surely this mischievousness was the perfect complement to the courage of maturity!

In this book, I am Great Grandmother Gill, in May 2054. I am a re-created artefact of all those strands. The threads were essentially tangled, unwise choices I made, based on presumption, delusion, imagination, fantasy and even fear. Later, converting these knots more effectively into hope, faith and sometimes inspired risk, my patterns and rhythms changed.

Who does that make me?

It makes me the person I have become, at eighty-nine. Perhaps not who I thought I would be; maybe someone better than I ever would have been. Certainly, better than I fundamentally believed I was. So what beliefs did I hold about 'me' for so many years that brought me here? What beliefs will sharp little Trea do well to uphold if she aspires to be everything she can be?

> "*God is watching us, God is watching us,*
> *God is watching us from a distance*"[2]

Trea gently sings as she concentrates on scribbling a fantastical feathered headdress.

Never liked that song! I think.

Any developed sense I now cherish of an intimately familiar and loving God is not exactly helped by the thought of Him peering over the lip of a cloud bank with sniper-like binoculars trained on us. As if she can read my thoughts, Trea looks up earnestly and appeals "*How can God be with us if He's distant?*"

That is how this account began.

I will explain God can be watching us from a distance and yet, with us; intimately involved with us in the creation or re-creation of our lives. He is with Jacob, simultaneously as He is with me or with you.

Three courses

I have three threads to weave for you. In fact, I'll present them as three courses to navigate. From them, I want to convey the complexity and depth of the testing and rewarding journey of maturing faith as a Christ follower mid-way through life at the turn of the millennium.

- The biblical story of Jacob
- A narrative canal journey
- And my own life lessons in strife distilled through Trea

1. The biblical story of Jacob

Jacob is a character I long felt ambivalence toward. Along with Esau, he was one of troubled twins born to Isaac, and the one grandson of Abraham that the Bible pays a great deal of attention to. Often self-obstructed by his characteristic scheming and deceit, the course of his repeatedly thwarted life is recorded in the biblical book of Genesis.

Casting a glance at the connections between Jacob's account and mine has been a source of comfort and discomfort for me. I think you will understand that when someone refers to your likeness in a famous character, part of you feels gratified and part of you feels a little offended. Truth is, we are all imperfect, and the imperfections are all there in glorious display in the Bible, both for our irritation and reassurance.

Here's the uncomfortable truth. I was the frustrated mid-lifer whose reliance upon self-will and human strength was beginning to wear thin.

Jacob is an object lesson of strife, discontentedness, and scheming. The name Jacob means *"he that supplants or undermines"*. In old English novels, we sometimes read about the archetypal spoiled young heir of an estate who has no regard for the value of his inheritance and spends it in wild living. Known as a *cad* or a *heel*, this reference directly originates from the fact that Jacob came out of the womb grasping the elder twin's heel. Jacob, the deceiver, was straining to obtain his elder brother's inheritance. So, Jacob is *grasping*, a man known for his schemes and tactics, designed to outwit others and live by intellectual advantage rather than his rightful position.

Great temptation may occur (when IQ gives the upper hand) to one who is gifted in strategic ways. Jacob's sharp mind was both his strength *and* weakness. He displayed all the potential and frailty that comes to a naturally gifted person. Indeed, he also had a role model in his mother who was cleverly frugal with the truth. She positively encouraged him to trick his father Isaac into mistaking him for Esau one fateful day.

Despite all of this, you can read of a direct reference to the house or tribe of Jacob in Jeremiah. This is a tribe descended directly from our deceitful anti-hero. God speaks restoratively through Jeremiah to the people of his day by powerfully illustrating the nature of His grace toward those of us who are just like Jacob!

God says, *"Who would dare to approach me unless he was invited?"*[3] By implication, you are meant to realise Jacob was *certainly* invited to approach God.

Would I be? *Would you?*

Well no, you would absolutely dare *not* (unless invited).

Remember, this was God people only encountered through the boundaries of Old Testament limitations. God was One who could not look at unrighteousness. By nature of His holiness, He would consume with fire, anything corrupted or defiled that had not been carefully atoned for by the meticulous laws of substitution and animal sacrifice.

How could someone with such a devious heart as Jacob imagine that he was acceptable in God's presence?

Yet this passage in Jeremiah suggests that "Jacob" (or *Israel*, as he had been renamed by this time) *is* welcome and acceptable. Because he has been invited, he *did* dare to draw near!

This whole passage is a series of promises to us today. We, who are God's children have been called by name to be restored, rebuilt, increased, honoured, established and delivered.

But, says the Lord, when I bring you home again from your captivity and restore your fortunes, Jerusalem will be rebuilt upon her ruins; the palace will be reconstructed as it was before. The cities will be filled with joy and great thanksgiving, and I will multiply my people and make of them a great and honoured nation. Their children shall prosper as in David's reign; their nations shall be established before me, and I will punish anyone who hurts them. They will have their own ruler again. He will not be a foreigner. And I will invite him to be a priest at my altars, and he shall approach me, for who would dare to come unless invited. And you shall be my people, and I will be your God.

(Jeremiah 30:18-22, TLB)

I find it fascinating that this passage begins by referring to the people's wealth and prosperity, their happiness and increase. It goes on to talk about less tangible things such as honour, security, and freedom. Finally, the climax is that their leader can draw near to God.

One of the features of modern life is that we are more concerned with material gain than quality of character and life. Least of all that we might know and have a relationship with God. Yet this is the very foundation of Israel's promised holistic prosperity. He says *"So, (because you are devoted to me) you will be my people and I will be your God"*, v22.

This relationship is the basis of "good fortune".

Good fortune is what Jacob was seeking when he grasped Esau's heel in the womb, when he tricked Esau into selling his inheritance for an urgently needed bowl of stew.

Good fortune was what he sought when he presented himself to Isaac in pretence as if he were his brother; to receive the one and only prayer of blessing that Isaac could grant.

Good fortune is what Jacob was hankering after when he ran from his family home to escape Esau's wrath, to find a wife and a get-rich-quick earning from his Uncle Laban.

It's what led Jacob to embark on some far-fetched genetic engineering that led to his flock of sheep prospering while Laban's diminished. For all its weakness, Jacob always defaulted to the familiarity of working by his wit. Finally, he was confronted with the inadequacy of standing in the power of his own strength.

Throughout a hard spell of labour under his wives' father Laban, Jacob was force-fed a dose of the same family trait of human connivance. This was the same kind of plotting that had already caused his original family members such heartache. Twenty years on, having gained wealth by his own natural power to scheme and outwit, Jacob was at the limit of his father-in-law's containment. He was fleeing again, in the vain hope of another new start.

It was years before Jacob began to sense that he could not live by his wits forever and expect to get away with it. At last, beginning to gain a more mellow appreciation of his own limitations, he complained to his father-in-law, bitterly.

> *"This was my situation: The heat consumed me in the daytime and the cold at night, and sleep fled from my eyes. It was like this for the twenty years I was in your household. I worked for you fourteen years for your two daughters and six years for your flocks, and you changed my wages ten times.*
> *If the God of my father, the God of Abraham and the Fear of Isaac, had not been with me, you would surely have sent me away empty-handed. But God has seen my hardship and the toil of my hands, and last night he rebuked you."*

(Genesis 31:40-42, NIV)

We see that despite Jacob's tortuously delayed insights into the gracious and patient heart of God behind the scenes, He waits. He allows us to learn and he looks after the things he badly wants us to inherit, eager to invest them just as soon as we are ready to handle them.

Jacob had been on the run for twenty years but how much more God still had to show him. When we find him in Genesis 31, Jacob is finally facing the consequences of his extensive striving. He faces what he believes will be an almighty showdown with his embittered father-in-law, who he abandoned in utter frustration taking both of Laban's daughters and the family jewels.

Laban's fury would have put an end to Jacob if it had not been for the restraint of the Lord upon him.

> "Laban said to Jacob, "What have you done? You've deceived me, and you've carried off my daughters like captives in war.
> Why did you run off secretly and deceive me? Why didn't you tell me, so that I could send you away with joy and singing to the music of tambourines and harps?
> You didn't even let me kiss my grandchildren and daughters good-bye. You have done a foolish thing.
> I have the power to harm you; but last night the God of your father said to me, 'Be careful not to say anything to Jacob, either good or bad.'
> Now you have gone off because you longed to return to your father's house. But why did you steal my gods?"
> Jacob answered Laban, "I was afraid, because I thought you would take your daughters away from me by force."

(Genesis 31:25-31, NIV)

The lesson of Jacob is that he lived by the power of his own might and strength. He was afraid, of what man could do to him, of what man could take from him. Of the twenty years since the day his own mother urged him to flee for his life, everything we see of his life is answered here, in this simple phrase, *"I was afraid"*.

Jacob reckoned up everything he met in terms of its relative power and force. This was how he judged himself and his own value. Inevitably such a mindset let him down at some point and even drove him to act rashly, selfishly and dishonestly.

2. A narrative canal journey

The second theme of the book is the journey of a narrowboat along the course of the English Leeds-Liverpool canal. This is a metaphor of life, punctuated with descriptive vignettes of the many passing, changing landscapes (or testing challenges). Imagine yourself with me. You are the passenger who learns to trust. You will learn how to travel with an assurance of safe arrival and to experience the richness of the journey as it unfolds.

We visit periodically along the course of the canal route and take stock from the crest of several different bridges. Jacob, Trea and I have transition point interjections and conversations from each one of these bridges. We explore these transitions of the journey through parallel seasons of our lives. These are told through the conversations I have with my great-granddaughter Trea and her many questions.

The great Chinese theologian Watchman Nee wrote of the transition of a person's "walk", from a place of self-determination to God-submission in his famous book *"Sit, Walk, Stand"*[4]. Every bridge in *As If* represents a point of transition in the life of a growing Christian. It also gives an opportunity to reflect upon the transformations in the life of Jacob, the famous Biblical character that I have the (dubious) pleasure of being familiar with.

Each part of the book introduces the watercourse at every bridge of transition. Each of the chapters tells the story of every subsequent lock and pound (the stretch of water between each lock). With each, is a check on progress, a blatant barrier and then after its successful negotiation, the narrowboat travels forward.

For example, when the Fight Bridge comes into view, it heralds the transition into the 3-rise staircase. It was a navigation disaster. I spent six years as a pastor. And to a degree, I relaxed into the journey, though the threat of doubt and fear was never far away.

Here was the supposedly beautiful local church 'dare2live'. Let's say it was a narrowboat, our very shiny, bright and freshly painted, twenty-first-century version of a local church. An evolving, devoted bunch of people who never let a doubt cloud the picture God gave them, at the birth of who they were and what they would do for Him.

It had been supposed to demonstrate what He could do for us. Instead, it was the climax of those fumbled attempts to enter and rise into the flight of things God promised.

This was a season of strife. It was the equivalent of the Leeds-Liverpool 3-rise staircase. As the narrowboat circled gently to the foot of this unique and formidable flight, I entered a confusing initiation into the art of lock negotiation.

I failed dismally.

After Sitting Bridge, the Staircase chapters (9-13) tell of lock after lock after lock that came with no resultant 'pound' or lock-free stretch of water - no freedom, no breakthrough, no apparent change; only the terrifying balance between the promise that we were one step nearer and the dread that we were locked in forever.

This was not one, not three, but the series of ascending Bingley 5-rise locks. As daunting as it is spectacular, such a rite of passage required an entirely different level of understanding, new principles and new depths of courage and conviction.

And I made a complete mess of it!

3. Life Lessons Through Trea

Thirdly, as Trea and I visit the renovated canal bridges in 2054, we take in the spiritual lessons of the life I lived sixty eventful years earlier.

As for Jacob, perhaps self-deception is the crux of my story too. Dreaming, imagining and scheming, sometimes self-delusion, blinded me from the facts. I met my own versions of Laban, and like Jacob, God had some lengthy, subtle, extensive and transformational lessons in mind for me.

Therefore, in 2002, I railed at the thought that God was giving Jacob's name as a foundational character, and a corresponding Scripture to base the launch of a church upon. I wouldn't even have wanted to name a son Jacob, never mind a church. But *dare2live* it was, after Jacob's ancient invitation described by Jeremiah.

We too were received, in drawing near. Only because we were invited. That was without doubt. Many doubted that we had been asked to do this. I have no doubt that we were invited. But with the passage of time and trial, we did not continue to trust that invitation.

"What are you?" is a question that I have paid a great deal of attention to, and I have a ready and watertight answer.

I decide - **I am a declaration.**

STANDING - BRIDGE

YOU SAY, "I WILL!"

CHAPTER 1
FROM WHERE I'M STANDING

Great Grandma Gill and little Trea visit the marina

"What are you Grami?" asks Trea, my seven-year old great-granddaughter.

She is in complete ignorance of the enormity of this simple question. We are sharing an ice-cream treat in the retro dairy creamery where historical narratives of the 20th Century rural and waterway industries are exhibited. Trea is wondering who I would choose to be, of any character in the entire world. I glance at her talented drawings of fantastic creatures and smile. Our leisurely setting and my characteristically philosophical interpretation of her question is an irresistible trigger for reflection.

Am I a product of what I did?
Who I knew?
Or where I went or what I desired?

She has me thinking, and while she entertains herself with animated drawings of *Specio* the morphing magician, I ponder at the answers I might give.

"What are you?" is a question that I have paid a great deal of attention to, and I have a ready and watertight answer.

I decide - **I am a declaration.**

"I am *Sought-After Dares*" I tease, "but that's another story"[1]

Tables are abandoned one by one. Brittle leaves scud around the industrial planking floor and the air begins to cool.

Trea and I pack away her colouring pens. I turn from my afternoon musings as we gather our items to return to the car. I had needed to rest. I balance my frame on the curved wall, leaning on the sun-warmed stone of the canal bridge, crusty with lichen. The bridge offers strength as I have weakened from my exertion of reaching this viewpoint. I take in the spellbinding view of the winding waterway picked out in the low afternoon sun.

A ribbon of gold snakes all the way back to the far horizon from where I have travelled.

Just as I remember it.

The rise of the canal era and its provision by those who first saw its potential for transport and prosperity was a feat of engineering vision. Those pioneers tackled topographical challenges and traversed stretches of countryside with their new transport strategy and refreshing approach to the needs of their time.

Our canal route sometimes winds with the natural geographical features, and at times cuts more directly from

East coast to West through the northern Lancashire-Yorkshire border.

It is a picture of life

The canal course is sometimes arduous, sometimes ruthless, incisive and forceful. Its waterways are always purposeful, often gentle and complementary to her contemporary transport systems. No natural force created her, she was placed there by one who saw and planned her potential and antagonised the terrain that she would traverse. Lined with clay waterproofing that preserves her integrity, she still effortlessly carries her precious cargo. In business or pleasure, she quietly leads the way.

Even now the waterways serve holiday makers and nature lovers with rich enjoyment and fulfilment. Tourists, such as Trea and me.

The final lock

Lancaster canal's circuitous route holds precious memories of lazy picnics and wildflower gathering, pony-spotting and bumpy towpath cycle rides. The spiritual life I began at this time, often mirroring its serendipitous bottle-green depths took on a more urgent and sinister turn at half point. In harmony with the industrial grey of the Lancashire Yorkshire towns, a frustration with the grinding pace and repetition set in.

At Forton, once a childhood village home of mine, the waterway of the Lancaster canal, motorway, the A6, and railway all converge, running parallel for a short span of their routes. Like unequally matched runners in a race, they travel briefly, at one, quickly dispersing in their own pace and style. I reflect on the uniqueness of my journey and those who ran with me, at least for some of the time.

Ordinary people

Who could have sensed the cost of compassion stirring in my ten-year-old heart? Witnessing an elderly man's cup of tea being spilled over in a busy café as he was jostled by an impatient customer, that shy 'me' agonised over whether it was appropriate to give him ten pence to buy another drink!

No one would have pointed out the insular and conscientious high school student, pushed toward exam success and the need to achieve the best results of all. Sacrificing popularity and peer acceptability, already far behind, I reached for the deceptive lure of personal achievement.

I mean there were successful people, and there were *ordinary* people, and we were ordinary ones. I came from a provincial, industrial birthplace. My parents' sincere attempts to better themselves, included a brief fling (and for my sister and me a thrilling spell in the Midlands and Norfolk). We remained ordinary.

Hardworking, comfortable and ordinary.

No one would have picked from amongst the masses, *my life*, the life of a prim Lancashire lass from an average lower-middle-class family in an industrial suburb of sixties Britain. No one would have noticed the self-conscious and introverted new girl adjusting again and again to new school and new dialect; first from Bury to the Midlands, to Norfolk and then the Lancashire Wyre.

The empty pursuit of striving for straight 'A's' would have led me into a blind alley of despair if I had not asked in ignorance yet hopefulness for my distant God to reveal himself to me. My eyes were opened to a revelation of a meaningful and valuable life that is in Jesus. At fifteen years old, I sensed a peace and joy that was indescribable.

This became a staying and keeping power in my life that would keep me focussed and sensitive to a call of differentness and uniqueness that would set me apart for a far-off investment aiming to bring hope for the hopeless, restoration to the broken and beauty to the rejected. I didn't have that language then (though I might well use it now) but it went *something* like that.

I was that insignificant teenager.
I was that conscientious but faceless National Health Service employee.
I was that obscure and insecure nurse.

Then, I became that over-worked and driven young mother who allowed her active desire to please God develop everything except her own family life and spiritual health. I was that frustrated pastor who saw people's promises and allegiances crumble to dust and watched them walk away from their place in her heart and soul.
I said I was a pastor.

I was also the fundraiser who toiled over multiple bureaucratic and fickle benefactors' criteria for success. I saw a mere 3% return on two years of needs analysis, business planning, and strategic direction.

I was the Centre Manager....
I was the Secretary....
I was the book-keeper....
I was.....
I was...
I was.

Just Who did I think I was?

As a pastor, I once, I steeled myself against the probable disappointment of a church member's teasing, empty promise. It was a 'millionaire's' tithe that had no basis of truth. I knew that God would allow me to wrestle with all such things until I somehow accepted the security of a place where there was no backup plan. He would wrestle until I had no possible solution to the need for finance, more team support and a fast disappearing reserve of personal energy.

This would be my call

I was an aspiring world-changer. I gave up a life that had been self-made and effort-filled in seeking every measure of success and honour. I gave it up to understand who God is and how He could mean what He had said I would do.

Knowing it would take me to the wall, when the life savings, endowment policy, and re-mortgaged equity ran out, I chose to leave my nursing and academic career in palliative care. Till then, I could only give the leftovers, because I had allowed my career to become a burden and a distraction. I told myself that resignation would allow me to attend to the 'larger task' of building the local church. Otherwise, I would never know if it would work.

But I continued to feel the wrench of people's departure, along with all the investment in them and supposedly through them. I was desperately and unsuccessfully looking for some compensation in every loss. Each was inexplicable to me within the permission and gift of an all-powerful and providential God. It was as if an imagined debt of explanation from God to me was building a thick wall between hope and expectation.

Borrowed faith

The time the concept of *'destiny'* messed with my worldview was when a preacher announced to a crowded room that we were *people of destiny*. It puzzled me *'How does he know that?'* I thought. I only knew what I saw and not what could be. Instead of being intrigued and aware of a positive shift in my self-belief, the encouragement-stirring hunger for reaching my full potential, I lurched into a frantic hunt for favour.

And that's when I borrowed someone else's faith to build a new vision of my future. I thought it was my vision. Most probably it was not. Maybe this is what Jacob did. Instead of dealing with the personal insecurities that were to dog his life for decades, he followed his mother who urged him to do better, run, seek and get the best he could for himself.

Trans-Pennine Faith

Many of my life's journeys have repeatedly traversed the two northern counties, clinging to the various cross-Pennine routes. As a child, I would rattle up and down the M62 from Lancaster to visit grandparents in Rochdale. Passing rivers and dam, I was enfolded in the night-time fairy-tale blanket of stars thrown across the Greater Manchester valleys on cosy Sunday night returns from Spotland Road and Grandma and Grandpa's warm fireside farewell. As a student, I relished the alternative perspective of the Lancaster via Leeds to Hull railway journey. And again, as an adult driver, I traversed the M62 from Hull to Lancaster, cutting through hillsides and inevitably hitting rain on the mid-western moors.

(Even now, I periodically speed past the same antique farmhouse cottage still clinging to the swathe of land between the east and westbound carriageways, resolutely and grimly defying everyone else's progress. I saw a news report once that celebrated the single-handed commitment of a twenty-something-year-old young woman who herds sheep here in her isolated anti-21st Century lifestyle).

We were onto something

My travelling reduced. It was punctuated now and again by a work-related foray into the Moors above Flockton, a visit to see my parents or an enthralling trip to absorb inspiration in our discovery of an emerging new breed church in West Yorkshire.

We were onto something. Yes, *we*. I was married by now. We were one of those couples that get noticed. Well, *he* got noticed, and I was attached to him. He was lean, six foot six, Afro-Caribbean and charming. Once, someone called us "*Beautiful people*".

I took that with a large pinch of salt!
Yet, we were awakening to a new comprehension and culture of destiny and hope.

If passion alone had been enough to take us into all that we beheld, we would have stormed ahead. If effort could have driven us, we would have travelled as far as its fuel tank could carry us.

Little did I know, we were not simply going to walk right into all that promise.

And that's the mistake I made.

We entered a season of exaggerated frustration and anguish It could have been avoided with a different approach to navigation. It was years before the vehicles of resilience and humility overcame the obstacles and bewilderment we encountered. My triumph in arriving here today came at a deceptively subtle high price, though it was one that every destiny traveller must pay.

Finally came the perspective lent to me by God that He wanted me to believe: to *simply see things as if they are, not as they might be.*

This was the fine difference between faith and fantasy, however altruistic the fantasy was. This was the difference between destiny and delusion.

Now I contemplate what emerged from the maelstrom of that mid-term fight of my life when I battled with His ways over mine. I was this dogged and self-deceived Christian, and I look back with hindsight to that revolutionary time of profound transformation. I was 40 and tired of doing it my way, tired of being a good girl, tired of doing the right thing and not getting the results I expected. I poked fun at my own mid-life crisis even while I knew that it was far more than a hormonal rite of passage.

God blessed the beginnings of my vulnerable honesty and humbled truthfulness. He exposed the pain and privation of my British cynicism and gave a recipe for deliverance from my introverted fearful self. As a lonely leader, within a marriage to an irritatingly bolder-than-sensible Caribbean, this meant a painful severance from my guarded persona, from my self-preservation and small-mindedness. I became honest to God and willing to face the blockages to my inner growth.

I failed, spectacularly

After failure there comes freedom. If you choose to call it what it is. By grace, there is protection from bitterness. Then, and sometimes after a long time of reorientation, *then only* do people draw together again to serve, without personal affront or mixed motive. Through a newly meaningful and personalised message and ministry, God can refine a people for Himself who show a tangible love to their communities and play out a sacrificial life upon the world stage.

Because they failed and admit it.

And I did, and I do.

Now I am aged. I scan the horizon and see a favour of God that has rested upon the latter half of my life. That's the bit after the failure. Through stubbornness and anguish, I found a new God–intimacy. What a dynamic relationship with the Father! From vain and fiercely resisted and protracted beginnings it grew. Through self-doubt, humbled, fumbled and misplaced endeavour I finally hit upon a world-changing message of transformation.

I have taken this to heart. And now I write of it freely.

The Craft of the Waterway, Spiritual engineering

Those untimely growth blockages are like locks in this waterway of life. We must pass through each lock to continue the journey. The locks are there because the land gradient rises or falls. Without the lock, the water cannot flow toward its destination. Without the engineered correction of circumstances or artificial manipulation of the law of gravity, the narrowboat is condemned to stay in the pound. Its destiny is contained at the extremity of its current location.

It may turn and go back, stagnate or succumb to a time of preparation in which it is equalised toward the next level of water. This is an elegant engineering solution brought to bear upon the problem. The craft of the waterway is stunning in its simplicity and parallels the work of God in our own predicaments. We are too clumsy and unwise to navigate otherwise. The Holy Spirit alone can forewarn and implement readiness when we co-operate with guidance from the instruction panel at the waterside, or with the personal help of the lock-keeper.

And many of us do put our hand in His, learning to trust and to pursue His principles in our life that lead to the next open stretch of water and liberty as we move forward in the strength of what He has taught us.

Faith that I would find faith

You may ask 'Was it in faith that you did this?' *It was in faith that I would find faith,* by taking myself out of the safe confines of a monthly salary, social standing, and prestige. And the pressing busyness that diverted my best efforts to give my life to this cause.

However, even after this, the anticipated flood of relief and blessing upon leaving work didn't flow. I took my endeavouring approach to life into church. He said that the government was upon *His* shoulders, yet it felt as though it was all on *mine.*

Perhaps every life, every valid testimony, has a 'Bingley 5-rise' staircase season. Incredibly, these seasons are built, yes *God–designed* to get us *through,* not to obstruct our passage.

They are a focussed transition point for accelerated height.

Lifting the water table of life

Looking back with the luxurious vantage of hindsight, I see what came beyond and despite all that. Now I enjoy deep and rich relationships that cherish and nurture one another. There is a beautiful trust and honour between my daughter and me, and awe at the privilege of producing a son with great wisdom, passion, and insight. Now we stand strong and courageous in a fearful and unstable world. We are full of faith for the things God has promised.

With hope against all hope, we hope and do believe in His deliverance.

Yes, in this bitterness of experience I found the call to *know Him*, sweetly drawing me. Knowing that it would take me to the end of myself, I asked for and finally received an emerging, amazing injection of personal faith that was given to me at a critical juncture in my journey.

This book promises to reveal a great secret, an open-*your*-lock-secret that is meant to be accessible and even familiar to you too.

Yet the enemy of your soul has made you disdainful or ignorant of its power. Upon my journey, I admit, its simplicity eluded me for many years.

Perhaps those around you whom you respect, from whom you seek counsel, advise you to cut your losses or take a flight into the sun? You cannot accept that your current fight is all in vain. When your fiercest critic beholds your downsized existence and misreads the process in operation, you swallow your defensive explanations. There is still no other option but forward even as you quake in fear at the potential loss and shame. Even as you relish a total fall back on the familiar and forgotten bliss of ignorance and self-sufficiency.

You cannot go back, and you are terrified to go forward.

Like an orienteer, who has found their co-ordinates but keeps looking around to make sure this is it.

As if it were the future

That's how it was for me when I had a glimpse of this future, *as if* I stood with God in the future, right here, on the crest of this bridge. It gave me an understanding of my present and released a new co-operation with Him during my brokenness.

Though I was a visionary, though I was imaginative and could call to the heart of those I spoke with, a depth of passion for serving and for loving, this was a new seeing. This was my heart awakening, an opening of the eyes *of my heart* enabling *me* to see because of the spirit of wisdom and understanding[2]. This was the gift of faith that is mine and yours in the measure to which we desire and is accorded to those who desire it, according to your need. Even according to your newly perceived need.

Futility is a lie

The lies of your tangible physical circumstances may scream at you, insisting to you *"I am real. I am your reality. I am your future! You are locked in, locked down!"* These prevailing thoughts prevent anything from changing because they avoid the belief that anything can change. The futility of life with such a perspective is a deception that smothers many lives. For me, this was a stronghold that defied identification for years. That was, until I found new 'present' appreciation of moments with my children. I discovered a new joy in other's taken-for-granted deep love and lifelong friendships of such depth and quality that outweighed my wildest dreams.

Incidentally, gloom may be a sign that your vision has become blocked or stuck in the past. Instead, an *As-If* mentality gives you the grounding of expectant faith, held fast by hope. This cultivates a tendency toward future-orientation, an attribute that lends itself to an *As-If* mentality.

As if it has all come true.
You can live at peace now with the fact that it will.

Then, you and I really live.
"As If", **has universal relevance**.

Each of us is uniquely called and created for a specific purpose. I was slow to understand but having grasped the hope to which I was called, from then on, I visualised myself here, standing from a perspective of completion and acceptance, revolutionising each remaining day. Watchman Nee reinforced this conviction with the simple explanation that faith is always rooted in the past[3].

In other words, hope in a certain future does rest on what God has already done, said and imagined. It indeed remains my growing and consuming desire to grow in my faith and trust in God.

Now we will explore this deeper, ongoing, maturing walk in faith that God desires for us all to experience. It goes far beyond that first deposit of saving faith. The maturing and growth of others' developing faith still is His top priority. Surely this is His highest desire for you?

> *"By faith Jacob, when he was dying, blessed each of the sons of Joseph, and worshipped, leaning on the top of his staff"*
>
> (Hebrews 11:21, NKJV)

From where I am standing

Leaning on this old canal bridge, the only thing I can do is worship. I am eighty-nine years old, chronicling a celebration of insights that both tantalised and tormented me during the formative years of my life and ministry. Those were the middle years of my prime that dangled on the edge of abandonment to God or disillusionment and mediocrity. Looking back from where I'm standing, who could have known all that I could dare to dream, imagine or conceive, would have happened like this. Who could have known? Who could have accepted that this would be my life? Who could have imagined these things?

That they would come to pass at all - if it had not been for that focussed mindset upon demolishing all strongholds of *"I can't"*, *"Who, me?"* and *"Who do you think you are?"*. I am smaller, older, weaker and, like Jacob, I am disabled by the fight I have fought. And the lesson I have learned is that He uses those who are dying to themselves and their own imaginations, ways, and techniques. In doing so, you have an awesome vantage of God and His wildest possibilities. You have something tried and tested to pass on and bless the next generation. And still, you have a faith that He continues the good work that He started, obstructed and then released.

Because God said it, you can do it.
Because He said it and you believe it.
You may be a believer, but do you *believe*?
How **will you do it?**

As far as He's concerned, **because He said it, you have already done it!**

Come on Trea, let's get back home, your mum will be wondering what on earth we are doing out here all this time!"

CHAPTER 2
CUTTING LOOSE

It is time to embark upon this new mode of transport. I have been handed the waterway guidance code and 'shown' the ropes. Papers are signed, and ignition key is in hand. I start to unwind the mooring ropes from the silver-paint tipped gleaming bollard. My co-pilot is already settled in the varnished wooden cabin.

We are both excited although a little nervous about the more challenging stretches of the waterway some distance afar. For now, the vista is wide and bright to the right. Occasional cows dot the distant rising grassland like errant splashes of black and white emulsion flicked carelessly onto a new carpet. On the left margins of the canal, purple loosestrife spears cross-hatch the edges of the water, bobbing as the gentle ripples of the stern hit the channel. Sprays of marshmallow white and pink yarrow wave in the damp hem of the towpath and green-leafed fronds encroach the headspace of any passing walkers.

I must discover where everything is stored. First, there is anything connected to sailing; equipment, windlass, lubricating oil, waterproofs, and moorings. There are essentials connected to the everyday domestic requirements of living, sleeping, cooking and eating on a boat. Notably, we are stripped of our usual variety of entertainments and preoccupations as we must exercise continuous vigilance and anticipation for the stretch of water ahead, monitoring progress against the passage of time and adjusting our rest stops accordingly. We have a few mishaps and miss a few home comforts too. However, after a couple of hours, things feel more familiar, and our thoughts turn to seeking refreshment.

Enchanted

For about two weeks after the momentous day in which I first grasped the spiritual truth of salvation, I bounced around in a bubble of delight and wonder. It was just a couple of months before my fifteenth birthday. This effect, my personal joy at the precious gift of Jesus' life was like the first embarkation of my hired narrowboat. I touched and feasted on all the features, quirky symbolism and colourful panels and furniture. It was all straightforward and functional. Efficiently compact yet ornate.

Inhabiting this unusual craft seemed self-explanatory and perfectly suited. Released from my moorings, I had entered a brand-new freedom and perspective that changed and unfolded with each passing hour.

I was curious, attentive and wondrous. These are childlike qualities and precious in His sight. How we so quickly slide from this position of receptivity to grace into a mistaken need to start earning its continued presence and favour. Like sparkling dust specks in a beam of light, such constant yet momentary favour cannot be collected, bartered or manufactured. It can be noticed, enjoyed and appreciated, drawn attention to and described.

If I hadn't been in the boat, I wouldn't have seen the views from the perspective of the boat. So why did I feel obliged to keep getting off and chasing these fleeting scenes? Already I was experiencing a challenge to my newly-forming trust. I needed to recognise that if He had invited me on this route, He was the one who knew when and what He wanted me to see and experience of the scenery and momentary encounters with animal, vegetable or mineral.

This was His invitation.
He is not capricious.
I did not, I do not, nor do I ever have to try to make anything happen.

Do you know this? Do you believe it?

The traveller's enjoyment is not just a response to the beauty of nature, cultural novelty or created art and architecture. The urge to explore and discover and absorb the experience of people and places is a picture of a spiritual truth. He has specific encounters, revelations, and realisations that are strewn across your life-path at just the right time and circumstance for you to grow in depth of knowledge of His goodness and His glory.

You simply choose to engage.
Yes, *you* choose.

You choose the path that He has chosen for you. Here is one of the thorniest concepts of the will and power of God that Christians have wrestled with for centuries. We understand that God has given us free will to reject or accept His love, His plan and His purposes for us. The traditional line goes something like this, *"If God did not give you free will, He would not be able to receive your love as a voluntary response to Himself. That would make us automatons"*. He wants a mutual and reciprocal relationship. So, He even gives us the power to reject Him and walk in darkness and ignorance.

Why would He risk such a thing when He knows we would be safer, happier, fulfilled and eternally secure with Him and not apart from Him? This is love, to let us go. We rail against the idea that He would watch us move off course and yet, every parent knows there is a moment like this that each one of their offspring will subject them to.

The point is, "Will they come back?"

Will you come back? This is when the real spirit of co-operation begins. It is the maturing of a relationship between the Lover and Beloved that is co-operative. Not resistant or even obedient but co-operative. As equal, even. How audacious is that? Audacious yes, but not presumptuous because He insists this is our privilege.

He does not ask for any more than a response. Not a copy or an alternative. You don't have to DO anything. This is perhaps the hardest thing for anyone to understand. And then, though you now understand that you cannot *get into* grace yet, you still feel the need to try to *stay* in it!

"Thou shalt do no un-commissioned works"

My first real pastor loved to joke that this should have been the eleventh commandment. When she first told me this, I did not grasp the emotional life-saving value she was handing me in those few words. I have outlived her by a few years already. I've lived long enough to realise that this could sum up the practise of all Ten Commandments in one fell swoop.

What a liberating way to live.

However, I suffer from a tendency to 'shoot from the hip'. It is a universal weakness that betrays a desire to be first, to be best, to survive and be approved. Just a little more reflection upon why I repeatedly allowed urgency to rob me of accuracy and, therefore a reward, would have served me well.

David was the one whom God called *"a man after my own heart"*[1]. He learned and later celebrated this principle of distinguishing between the natural urgency to 'do' and the more patient conviction of carefulness in 'how to do it'. Both approaches were showed publically in two different expressions of passion to glorify God. David's motives were pure on both occasions,

His first attempt to return the Ark of the Covenant to Jerusalem was fated by carelessness and rash presumption. The second attempt was successfully and forensically executed in a humble procession showing absolute dependence and attendance to the direction of the God of Israel.

And David knew

In 2 Samuel 5; (9 and12) David became the King over all of Israel, marching upon Jerusalem and conquering the invading Jebusites. The city, also known as Zion was captured and David re-named it the City of David. How vain you might think. Yet in verse12 we see why David had such confidence to do so.

> *"And David knew that the Lord had established him as King over Israel and had exalted his kingdom for the sake of his people Israel"*
>
> (2 Samuel 5:12, NIV).

Such conviction is a heavenly gift and indeed the lifeblood of the success of a God-inspired mission. We must operate through faith, by grace and not self-will, vanity or misplaced hope. None of us are necessarily aligned with this conviction 100% of the time. In fact, the next season after this conquest, David moved into presumption. Asking the Lord for guidance about every move (2 Samuel 5:19 and 22), this time he made the mistake of acting on his own good intentions. He slid from sensitivity to the touch of God's hand to having a good idea. It turned out to be a disastrous move.

David caught up in the delusion of his apparent infallibility failed to grasp the difference between human urgency and divine revelation.

> They set the ark of God on a new cart and brought it from the house of Abinadab, which was on the hill. Uzzah and Ahio, sons of Abinadab, were guiding the new cart 4 with the ark of God on it, and Ahio was walking in front of it. 5 David and all Israel were celebrating with all their might before the Lord, with castanetsharps, lyres, timbrels, sistrums, and cymbals.
> 6 When they came to the threshing floor of Nakon, Uzzah reached out and took hold of the ark of God, because the oxen stumbled. 7 The Lord's anger burned against Uzzah because of his irreverent act; therefore God struck him down, and he died there beside the ark of God.

> (2 Samuel 6:3-7, NIV)

Because of the judgement, God brought upon Uzzah who, without thinking steadied the cart, a new fear of God fell upon David. He had sensed the need to power **every** action and strategy out of the conviction and directional gift of the Holy Spirit. Three months on, after a period of undoubted reflection and soul searching, David realised that now he could complete his aborted mission with God's blessing.

In a remarkable blend of cautious progression and exuberant abandonment, he led the procession of the Ark of the Covenant back to its home in the Tent of Meeting. His inhibited wife, Michal, was mortified at what she saw as exhibitionism and public humiliation. David confirmed his painful life lesson about grace. It is clear he would never forget it when he responded,

> *"It was before the Lord, who chose me rather than your father or anyone from his house when he appointed me ruler over the Lord's people Israel – I will celebrate before the Lord. I will become even more undignified than this, and I will be humiliated in my own eyes"*
>
> (2 Samuel 6: 21-22, NIV)

David rejected *her* rationale for humiliation as unjustified because he had been about the Lord's work *of belief*. Not merely good intention or even selfish ego as she had judged. Now he proceeded in life with new awe and assurance; slowly, deliberately and worshipfully. This took David to a new level of abandonment and intimacy. He was not about to be chastised for it as ridiculous.

I wrote once in my journal after reflecting on these two accounts,

> *"There is a warning in this that 'carts' such as funding initiatives may carry the heart and vision of the church and though they may supply the resources to fulfil it, they carry it out of the scope it was intended for"*
>
> (30th January 2002)

It was needful that I exercised caution during my own balancing act - my mission to secure available funding for the church without compromising her mission. In the modern landscape of opportunity to apply for and secure charitable support, I knew that the pursuit could be a significant distraction. Yet it held so much promise.

The kind of projects that are on God's heart also happen to be socially valuable.

Of course, they are.

However, in any politically correct framework that determines criteria for secular funding, agencies do not easily award their resources if a church will be handling them. The fact that a faith organisation is awarded such finance may mean that someone has chosen convolution and legalism in applying the rules. I didn't want to do that, and so the whole experience was one of repeatedly bitter frustration, disappointment, and discouragement.

What is your work?

The distinction between human initiative (works) and the spirit is made by the gospel writer John - a point as counter-cultural then as it is this century. In John 6, after Jesus had ministered to the crowd of followers gathering to him at Galilee, the next day they followed him in boats to the opposite shore wondering how he had travelled there without a vessel overnight. He chastised them for their motives in chasing him for the food he had provided rather than for His own presence. Jesus pointed out that they were more interested in the fruits of their labour than in concerning themselves about the value of the labour itself. Predictably, and for all our benefit, they asked,

> *"What are we to do to, that we may [habitually] be working the works of God? [What are we to do to carry out what God requires?] Jesus replied, This is the work (service) that God asks of you: that you*

*believe in the One Whom He has sent [that you cleave
to, trust, rely on, and have faith in His Messenger].*

(John 6:28-29)

What is your work? It's this.
To believe.

Is that it? Surely there's more demanded than that?
And, of course, there is much more you and I can give.
But first - the foundation of all work is to believe.

Your *only* work is to believe. And what a work this is. So
often I would rather figure out, agonise over and run straight
into a challenge than to first wait, consider and ask of Him
"What would you have me do here?"

This impatience (in fact pride) has taken me down many a
dead end, or, at best, around some expensive detours. These
detours were costly in that I wasted years of precious time,
packets of energy and unspotted opportunities. Thank God
that hope, if not time is an infinite commodity and today
you and I can always start from where we are.

So now we know that un-commissioned work is anything
based in unbelief; lacking in grace, favour-less and inefficient.

In the book of Ephesians, Paul expanded upon something
he called 'the mystery of Christ' summed up in the famous
phrase,

*"For it is by grace you have been saved, through
faith—and this not from yourselves, it is the gift of
God –not by works, so that no one can boast"*

(Ephesians 2:8-9, NIV)

31

There is a need for revelation rather than heritage endowed rights, work or activity ruled by law, tradition or human urgency as inspiration.

Paul appealed to the church at Ephesus about this disruptive good news. In Chapter 3 he built upon a previous argument that Gentiles are now as able as Jews to access relationship with God the Father, by one Spirit, He called this fact,

> *"the mystery made known to me by revelation"* (v2).
> *It is in Him, and through faith in Him, we may approach God with freedom and confidence"* (v12).

Just as David did.

Once David was held by a misconception; an enchantment with the blessings that characterised his life and conquests. He had to have the spell that he could do anything without utter dependence upon God, broken.

The same earnest desire for imparting this humble understanding runs through all of Paul's letters.

> *"My purpose is that they may be encouraged in heart and united in love, so that they may have the full riches of complete understanding, in order that they may know the mystery of God, namely Christ, in whom are hidden all the treasures of wisdom and knowledge"*
>
> (Colossians 2:2-3, NIV)

Indeed, he despaired when the Galatian people corrupted their precious new revelation of complete acceptance through faith. They had swallowed the lie that they had to attain to their goal of salvation through human effort, compelling Paul to ask *"Who has bewitched you?"* (Galatians 3:1, NIV)

Spiritual Intimacy- not bricks and mortar

An American preacher, Robert Hotchkin[2], reiterated these ideas for me once at a conference I attended. He said that Kingdom progression is as much about relationship as it is in our efforts or the construction of a mansion in a heavenly destination. The Hebrew tradition of building a new marital home as an extension of the father's house is that which Jesus referred to when he told the disciples on the eve of His death *"I am going away to prepare a place for you"* (John 14:3). The deepest intimacy of relationship, consummation, begins in the Father's house.

I was 50 years old and a little jaded and bored in a season of my journey I describe as a long stretch of water without landmarks or scenic interest. There hadn't been much apparent growth in my unremarkable life. I was almost scared of meeting the next lock because it seemed such a long time since I had risen to any spiritual challenge other than perseverance.

His insights helped me to relax, prepare, notice and anticipate progress both in the transitions and between them.

Our safe and purposeful passage along this life-canal is measured not merely in the distance taken but also carried by our weight of character in the water-filled depth of His channel or His Being. Reliant upon a constant source of water from the heights of the mountain reservoirs and streams, we steer, direct and energise the vessel of our faith under the prescribed routes and options He has laid out for us.

We choose to be taken, and yet we are led in advance.

This chapter has been one of those that I had more difficulty with and one of the last few to be completed in this volume. Also, frustratingly, over the same few months, I have felt inadequate trying to explain the dilemma of free will to an agnostic friend. So, finding the following verse has blown me away with the possibility that God is much keener to 'have His arm twisted' than I realised. In fact, I wonder, *'Is He really even as dependent upon our intercession as I think?'*

> *The king's heart is like channels of water in the hand*
> *of the LORD;*
> *He turns it whichever way He wishes.*
> *²Every man's way is right in his own eyes,*
> *But the LORD weighs and examines the hearts [of*
> *people and their motives]*
> (Proverbs 21:1-2)

I believe that He loves to engage with our intercession, but that the motivations for our prayers and of the subjects of our prayer are what moves Him. What we need to pray is for insight into those things that please Him and will inevitably be the course of action He wishes to direct us in. Again, this is a sophisticated, interdependent relationship based dynamic. Not a slot machine or instruction manual. It is by grace and not works (or the rules by which we work).

Cross-section view

To take a liberty, I will re-interpret the great chapter of the trinity of interdependence between God the Father, Jesus the Son and the Holy Spirit in John chapter 14.

It is that of a cross-section diagram of the canal in its threefold construction of

1. the excavated channel
2. the clay lining,
3. and the watercourse poured into it

Picture 1: Diagram of a Brindley style construction of canal (cross section)

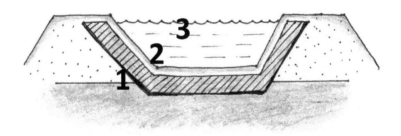

God the Father so loved the world, He dug out a course back to His original purpose and destiny for all mankind[3]. He gave His Son who was broken, mangled and pummelled like the clay formed into the waterproof canal lining. He made watertight, the salvation of all those who believe. Then as a guarantee and deposit of the heavenly blessings to come, He sealed this channel of clay with the Holy Spirit, additionally pouring out a further secondary measure of spirit into it (a baptism of the Holy Spirit).

Now this vessel, your life can be lifted and transported from one degree of glory to another with the passage of each lock and pound. Cut loose from the moorings that seem to hold you safe and tight, your sins of comfort and familiarity that prevent any progress or advance have been removed.

Hotchkin spoke of the fact that we can become so fixated on the promise of mansions in heaven that await us, we miss the more profound truth of the teaching of John 14 which is that we live in this Kingdom of God even now. Through the relationship we have entered, we inhabit an interim space of eternal communion. This is what happens within the canal lock. It is the space between one plane and another, the overlap of the two circles of heaven and earth in the unfolding Kingdom of God.

This is illustrated in the transition of the narrowboat from one water level to another. Paul described it in this way.

"To this end I labour, struggling with all His energy, which so powerfully works in me"

(Colossians 1:29, NIV)

Bringing together heaven and earth we are living in that advancing edge of Kingdom extension. This is the place where spiritual truth outworks its disciplining of the soul. Here we learn our lessons through the buffering of body and the spirit. The soul is the interface of these and the place where the enemy 'plays games' and we respond accordingly.

For though we walk in the flesh [as mortal men], we are not carrying on our [spiritual] warfare according to the flesh and using the weapons of man. 4 The weapons of our warfare are not physical [weapons of flesh and blood]. Our weapons are divinely powerful for the destruction of fortresses. 5 We are destroying sophisticated arguments and every exalted and proud thing that sets itself up against the [true] knowledge of God, and we are taking every thought and purpose captive to the obedience of Christ, 6 being ready to punish every act of disobedience, when your own obedience [as a church] is complete.

(2 Corinthians 10:3-6)

We show and declare the reality of eternal Kingdom in the slime and sludge of this messy temporal transition place.

We learn to look for the help and guidance of the Lockkeeper, to read the signage at the gate mechanism. We learn to look out for co-travellers and passers-by to make the best use of every situation for all concerned. We use the lock gates to drain or fill, for maximum benefit to all. Attacked in a cavalier fashion without recourse to the help and the principles of the etiquette of the canal, we eventually recognise that everything we do in our own strength requires twice the effort. No, we take the lead from the One who,

> "being in very nature God, did not consider equality with God something to be grasped, but made Himself nothing, taking the very nature of a servant

(Philippians 2:6-7a, NIV)

So, with these thoughts and insights about humility, mutual consultation and interdependence between ourselves and the Godhead, and even between and within the Triune God Himself, we are prepared for the cruise ahead.

Let's tackle this series of ascents and descents within the route of the waterway of life. They and we are here for a reason.

FIGHTING - BRIDGE

YOU ASK, "WHAT IF?"

"So Jacob was left alone, and a man wrestled with him till daybreak.

When the man saw that he could not overpower him, he touched the socket of Jacob's hip so that his hip was wrenched as he wrestled with the man.

Then the man said, "Let me go, for it is daybreak."

But Jacob replied, "I will not let you go unless you bless me."

The man asked him, "What is your name?"

"Jacob," he answered.

Then the man said, "Your name will no longer be Jacob, but Israel because you have struggled with God and with men and have overcome."

Jacob said, "Please tell me your name." But he replied, "Why do you ask my name?" Then he blessed him there.

So Jacob called the place Peniel, saying, "It is because I saw God face to face, and yet my life was spared."

The sun rose above him as he passed Peniel, and he was limping because of his hip."

(Genesis 32:24-31, NIV)

Trea has a tantrum

"Grami, why are we stopping here?" asks Trea.
"I just want to take a moment", I respond. *"This was a very significant place for me. I just want to remember."*
"But I want to go home now!" she retorts.
"Give me a little time", I insist.
"What did you do here?" Trea asks.

My mind has returned to the day I wrestled over the dawning of a horrible truth that I could not believe about the course of life I had set myself. It was going to be a shameful climb-down. I was back in my office of distressed sea-green woodwork, a 1990's décor trend. Cloistered away from the oblivious family group next door, it took just a few momentous minutes. The insistence I had carried for years, that breakthrough was coming, before God and any enquirer, fell hard like a heavy curtain.

It was the unveiling of a plaque announcing the end of an era of wrestling.

Trea won't let her interruptions go and threatens to drop her favourite dragon toy over the bridge if I do not break off from my musing. It dangles precariously and almost with a mind of its own, slips at the clumsy adjustment of her fingers as she attempts to refresh her grip. Dragon plops into the weeds and bobs gaily for a few moments before the weight of her soaking pulls her fibrous body under the surface. Trea had intended the threat to be a test of my nerves. Unfortunately for her it had all too easily, become a fact and one that she would have to absorb as a childish though significant self–inflicted loss.

It had been a brief showdown for all concerned, nevertheless defining and necessary.

Understandably Trea bursts into tears. These sobs turn into quiet heaving, sighing and sulking. Finally, acquiescing that it would not be a worthwhile tradeoff to attempt to dredge up the soft toy and carry its murky body home for a half-hearted restoration she breaks her gaze from the surface bubbles.

She has already learned an essential lesson of letting go, of cutting her losses,

Something I had struggled with right here on this bridge!

What if I had been more determined?

Or what if I had been less stubborn?

What if I had nearly got there? If I had unknowingly turned back at the very moment everything might have changed?

What if I had wasted my life?

CHAPTER 3
REASON - A GREAT SERVANT
BUT A POOR MASTER

I start to revise my handbooks and miss the evening's glorious sunset as I leave the steering to my mate, retreating into the cabin to prepare for the future challenge.

A sense of accomplishment rises within me as I assess that I have covered some distance of the unfolding journey. But this confidence is short-lived. I know that ahead lies a collection of locks. From the oak woods of the Aire Valley and the successfully negotiated Field Locks, the vessel skims through yet another bridge straddling Shipley. Steeply rising banks meet the famous mills and incline further up to the moors. Feeling secure and safe in the crook of the cool wooded glen, I traverse the Aire aqueduct and then negotiate the Dowley gap locks with satisfaction, seeing little from the narrowboat of the town it bisects. Jetties frequent the water's edge and pubs appear, a discarded can bobbing in the water. The construction of a yet unoccupied waterside development skirts a freshly railed pavement. Raw countryside gives way to tamed suburbian recreation and lifestyle. I feel intrusive and conspicuous.

As if to warn of impending opposition, the distant hum of road traffic crescendos as the waterway turns to parallel the busy Skipton route only to find my first challenging obstacle, a three-rise staircase of locks. For this inexperienced boat-handler, it arouses shock and a creeping sense of inadequacy.

The Lock of Reason

Either purposefully or more usually, by sub-conscious default programming, I allowed myself to be directed, empowered or even locked down and shut in by the definition of my belief systems. I spent most of my Christian life led by my mind. In the process, I denied my intuition or spiritual leading.

Psychologists have long agreed that every preceding mental belief determines an arising feeling and consequent action or behaviour. These behaviours shape the habits and character of a lifetime which themselves compound the originating beliefs. The power of the internal mental commentary and especially of audible words spoken from such a script is undisputed. These can be known as self-talk or self-fulfilling prophecies, and such patterns of entrenched thinking can be called a stronghold. The development of a stronghold is then set for positive or negative effect in our lives. In all areas of prominent achievement or spectacular failure, the outworking of the original mental image is the principal creative and determining factor.

Far more common is the middle ground of average mediocrity, where most humans experience a minimally taxing and satisfactory life. Or they exist in frustration and resignation at the challenging disadvantage they perceive themselves to be born to. But God is no respecter of persons, and this means each one has the capacity to grow out of such containment, whether it be a self-limiting belief or an externally obstructed position in life.

The key to any hope of change is the power of the mind to become its own creator.

We are made in the image of God and have an amazing capacity to think well of ourselves and our future. The Bible affirms this God-endowed view of humans.

> *"Now to Him who is able to [carry out His purpose and] do superabundantly more than all that we dare ask or think [infinitely beyond our greatest prayers, hopes, or dreams], according to His power that is at work within us"*

> (Ephesians 3:20)

This is our limitless potential if we engage our mental powers with confidence and only according to His power at work within us. There are many other publicised frameworks of positive thinking offering a way of escape from an ordinary and futile life. However, these are limited. Our imaginations are powerful but latent power can be counter-productive. The same creative processes activating all the powers of the imagination can also counterfeit or may even short-circuit truth, envisioning a deceptive or even fearful future that terrifies rather than inspires and compels.

Sometimes faith turns into fear

Faith and fear are very similar in origin though poles apart regarding their effect. We have been gifted with *such* colourful powers of intelligence. They can and should be celebrated and applied to the benefit of God's kingdom in wealth creation, research, team leading, literary, artistic and scientific pursuits to name only a few.

I am passionate that intellectual excellence because of great education and training in critical and clear thinking is as vital a gift to the church as any profession. It is a tool for family wisdom, domestic harmony, and lasting community impact. It is essential that Christians are articulate not only in their defence of, but particularly, their innovation in the faith.

Yet Reason is a great servant but a poor master

Earlier in chapter 2, I shared the lesson of wrangling between faith and works - that whole deal of recognising when one has stepped out of grace and into effort. That was about *self-effort*. In chapter 5, *self-will* gets some attention. Now here, the point is that we cannot allow *self-reason* to become our god. Powers of reasoning must always come under the authority of our spiritual nature. If the soul-powered and prideful mind rises with insubordination above its spirit-leader, it will be felled.

This was the case, in the prideful downfall of Nebuchadnezzar, the Babylonian King. Nebuchadnezzar had a dream that God had given to warn him his pride would cost him dearly. Nebuchadnezzar failed to appreciate that God and not his own strength was his source of success. One day as the King surveyed the prosperity of his life, he lost all sense of perspective that God had tried to warn him about through Daniel's interpretation. When Nebuchadnezzar fatally attributed all the success and power to his own ability, God brought the earlier warning judgement to pass, saying *"The kingdom has departed from you"* (Daniel 4:31)

Nebuchadnezzar entered a seven-year period of humbling.

"Let him lose his mind and get an animal's mind in exchange,"

(Daniel 4:16, The Message)

"Let his mind be changed from that of a man and let him be given the mind of an animal, till seven times pass by for him,"

(Daniel 4:16, NIV)

Nebuchadnezzar suffered a seven-year season of obscurity until he announced with the wisdom of this experience, that the King of heaven's works,

"are all faithful and right and Whose ways are just. And those who walk in pride He is able to abase and humble."

(Daniel 4: 37)

Secret tools in the arsenal of heaven

Weapons of effective spiritual warfare require humility. They insist that we *by-pass* reasoning and logical processes. Such reasoning may become a tormenting deception that you can *'sort it'* or that you can *'work it out'*. Only through humility, can revelation rather than self-determination have its transformative impact into our lives.

One tool is the New Testament teaching and practice of speaking in tongues

This requires a child-like trust in believing that the articulation of words with no intellectual meaning, is laced with power and spiritual relevance. The language of spiritual tongues is no mystery to God, merely to our human minds. If I subject the activity of a heavenly discourse to any filter of existing knowledge I possess I am limiting its potential. However, if I remove the filters of prior learning and finite human understanding, I am choosing to co-operate with God's higher spiritual and mysterious power.

Here's another tool.

Loving beyond Reason

Loving beyond reason is to love without waiting for a reason to reciprocate. Let's call it the windlass that opens the lock mechanism you are about to enter! There's a popular film 'Pay it Forward'[1] that plays powerfully with this concept.

I define *loving beyond reason* as a philosophy of seeing life **as if** it has already unfolded. This requires the ability to believe. It believes that the God who has created all things, all days, all reasons, all hopes and all dreams, is there at their fulfilment and their incubation.

Seeing and agreeing with this is a mental activity. However, the imaginations must be Spirit-led and not vain imaginations, doubts or man-made, presumptuous delusions. Many emerging thought-leaders urge the cultivation of a healthy thought-life. They claim to release more profound potential and stir attractive energies through affirmations, vibrational power, and mental disciplines. These practices do indeed release a certain power and influence. Nee warned of the dangers of this, calling it counterfeit spirituality, in 'The Latent Power of the Soul'[2].

The soul comprises of a tripartite connection of the mind, or reason; the heart, or seat of emotion and the origin of decision, the human will.

Christians often call the process of distinction between evil, human or God-initiated thoughts, the battle of the mind.

While the power of the soul can be cultivated by practises such as willpower, meditation, and affirmation, the power of the spirit belongs only to the Christian. Anyone who has not become born again is not born of the spirit, their spirit is dead, and their life is mortal, directed by the human soul. Once raised to life in Christ, that deathly state now works its way out and through the soul, the mind, emotions and will as the Christian exercises spiritual authority over these domains.

Surely this is what Paul meant when he wrote of his longing,

> "that I may know Him [experientially, becoming more thoroughly acquainted with Him, understanding the remarkable wonders of His Person more completely] and [in that same way experience] the power of His resurrection [which overflows and is active in believers], and [that I may share] the fellowship of His sufferings, by being continually conformed [inwardly into His likeness even] to His death [dying as He did"

> (Philippians 3:10)

Spiritual birth brings a supernatural and godly rather than soulish power. It is an endowed life-force of truth and discernment that now begins to authorise, rule and validate or eradicate these otherwise soulish practices. The Holy Spirit is free to operate through the restored human spirit as rivers of living water flowing from the innermost being, the spirit. Then on into the inner man (the soul) He flows, always at the behest of the human vessel's will or permission. The Holy Spirit tests and curtails or releases each thought, feeling and action through a straightforward filter.

The Flow Filter

The filter of spiritual prompting is to gauge whether something is beneficial even if it may be permissible. Our mistake is often that we relegate the *beneficial* below what is permissible or below what seems reasonable.

Those who are not born again cannot operate in this way even if they can apply the same principles for life. They can only do so in their own limited soul strength. Mistakes are inevitable. The temptation is to draw strength from other sources to counterfeit the desperate need to conquer this human condition. These may be sources such as popularity, amassing wealth or power, even conscious receptivity to demonic sources of power through deceiving philosophies and agreements or occult practices.

For Christians, ability to distinguish truth from deception by recognising the origin of a thought or impulse is one of the earliest and unremitting features of their relationship with God. They can tell the difference between the good things of life being the wonderful side benefits of a prospering soul rather than an absolute requirement for happiness.

Reason is a great servant but a poor master

Before I learned to submit my greatest strength of analytical thinking and endless questioning to this filter, it was also my greatest weakness. What should have been simple became complicated and confusing.

This is simplicity; the power of the Holy Spirit to test the source of all things through our spirit. Therefore, we know the value or risk each element poses to our integrity of character.

I always thought I had to *understand*, to accept a truth and surrender to it.

In fact, He doesn't ask us to understand but to trust. This has been my biggest battle of all. I winced at the familiarity of the sentiment of this quotation when I read it recently.

"You can have the peace that passes all understanding when you give up the right to understand"[3]

To trust, we can exercise our spirit by tuning into His. We need not apply reason at this point. In fact, this is where many become hung up on doctrinal differences and apologetic flair.

A simple testimony is enough.

Reason is much more compliant on the far side of Trust

On the far side of trust, reason rests with confidence beneath the masterful gaze of spiritual understanding. Robust reason now has space to breathe and stretch. It is happiest as a servant. Yet we have made it the ineffectual and uneasy master of our fateful self-deception.

So, the first thirty years of my Christian life I would say that my *soul-strength* was my mind. This is to say, my absolute temptation and tendency to self-effort and, therefore, weakness was the arena of my mind. My mind was fertile, active, selfish and suggestive. Prone to nightmares as a child, I was introspective, self-pitying and even within an established faith, regularly entertaining doubt and allowing myself to become intimidated by circumstance.

Each of us has an area of strength with the potential for it to become our Achilles heel (or Jacob's heel). Mine is my mental agility. Just as it allows me to enjoy contemplation and debate, it leads me down alleys of fanciful imagination and self-delusion that mean I sometimes struggle to distinguish between an actual memory or a fabrication.

I sometimes tie myself up in frustrating knots of mental fatigue. Your battle might be with your physical strength or agility. You have a similar capacity to overreach and excel in feats of strength or endurance. This might occasionally tempt you to smash a personal best and in doing so, trip, tear a muscle or break a bone.

Someone else may have a strong tendency to 'follow their heart' which is a cliched way of saying that their decisions tend to be emotionally biased. Of course, you know how fickle emotions can be from one day to the next, especially where hormones are fluctuating.

These may all be stereotypes, and I mention them with caution. They are not meant to be race, sex or personality typesets. As a teacher who loves to assist learners in their personal growth, I conduct personality, gifting and passion assessments[4] that give strong clues as to what a person's optimal position and function may be in a community, church or team.

Even so, these assigned 'types' with all their manifest strengths and weaknesses must then come under the rule and authority of the spirit of the person. Then, the power of the spirit interfaces with both the strength and weakness of the soul. The soul prospers only when it is submitted to His rule and reign. The arena of human strength and weakness is redeemed into the glory and image of Christ. In a posture of worship, everyone can reflect one of seven billion facets of Him.

> *"Therefore I urge you, brothers and sisters, by the mercies of God, to present your bodies [dedicating all of yourselves, set apart] as a living sacrifice, holy and well-pleasing to God, which is your rational (logical, intelligent) act of worship. And do not be conformed to this world [any longer with its superficial values and customs], but be transformed and progressively*

changed [as you mature spiritually] by the renewing of your mind [focusing on godly values and ethical attitudes], so that you may prove [for yourselves] what the will of God is, that which is good and acceptable and perfect [in His plan and purpose for you]."

(Romans 12:1-2)

Could you love beyond reason?

I have shown here that to relegate reason is to sacrifice the perceived need for understanding. Next, we learn that to love is to extend oneself generously without waiting for or needing emotional prompting.

CHAPTER 4

EMOTION - DENY THE FEAR
AND FLUNK IT ANYWAY

With a mild sense of panic, I wait anxiously for my partner to take the tiller and jump onto the kerb to mount the stone steps to the beam. That's when the craft all but grinds to a halt and slides between the slimy green walls of the empty pound. There is always the choice of alighting the simple metal ladder and abandoning my craft but to do that will choke the progress of many others in my wake. I am captured by obligation and inevitability, arrested, stopped and then, incredibly enabled.

The Lock of Emotion

If I had to identify the point at which the journey became wearing, I would have difficulty. More likely is the fact that years of knocks to my self-confidence took an accumulative toll. I realised this was necessary because in breaking down my self-confidence I was building up my God-confidence.

I believe God would have relieved the compounding difficulties much earlier if I had allowed Him to take much better care of them than I could.

Each setback or delay was a new lock in the waterway, put there for two reasons

- to allow me to develop my lock opening skills

- and to enable me to attain a new level of trust.

Instead, I saw them as frustrations, personal attacks and undermining criticisms that seeped into my soul, jading and fading the endpoint vision I had heralded.

Progress as a Christian seemed evident. Principles put into practice had worked well for me overall for over twenty years. My life journey paralleled the challenge of navigating a rising waterway. Each periodic lock with its neutral pool of water linking one chamber to the next was a wonderful picture of God's holding place in between seasons of life, a healing space or a waiting and training school.

However, the demands of simultaneously learning and leading as an example and guide were strength-sapping.

Emptying yourself

The paradox of being poured out on behalf of a cause, and yet protected from mingling and loss of self, are represented by the linked and interdependent pools of the multiple lock staircase. These are remarkable feats of engineering and to observe their ascent by others is a fascinating experience. However, there is no room for mistakes without significant water loss or inconvenience. There are designated opening times for passage and only when the help of the lock keeper is available.

Progress must be thought through much more than one step ahead.

Strategically: not emotionally.

Emotional indication, not instruction

This presence of the lock keeper as your assistant, your guide and as the one who greets you periodically along the journey is limited to time and season. It may be a wise friend or pastor, a parent or media accessible teacher. However, your life source and companion, the Holy Spirit is in the boat with you, and you are never too early or too late for His help.

Being fearful of, excited about or intrigued by something are various kinds of emotional experience. When your faith is determined by the temperature of your emotional life, (whether you feel passionate or not at all) you are being led by your emotions. Nevertheless, emotions are a gift, a blessing and a gauge as to how well the soul is prospering. Essentially, they should be an indicator and not the instructor.

In other words, we still have a choice how to respond to emotions and can master, release, or experience them in a balanced and healthy way. We all differ as to how they might need to come in line with the authority and will of God. Some of us are liberated and comfortable with expression without it being all-consuming and destructive. Others may have more trouble recognising and expressing emotions which can then become translated into dysfunctional behaviours and habits.

Some may be so led by their prevailing emotion, one could say they are dictated to rather than alerted by feelings. This is as dangerous as it is to be impervious to emotion or unable to express it. Like our capacity to reason, the feelings we are designed to experience are also intended to come under the rule of our spiritual or inner control, as led by the Holy Spirit. If either we deny or excessively delight in our emotions, we are doomed to suffer their excess. Then traits such as anger, depression or hedonism take hold of our life.

Emotions are valuable and powerful if we understand how to handle them. Again, the canal lock offers a wonderful picture of how we may harness them rather than be at risk of stagnation on the one hand or overpowering rushes of dangerous instability at the other.

For instance, I was affected the morning I planned to complete this chapter. Several debits were taken from my bank account overnight including an extraordinary annual payment pushing things beyond my overdraft limit. I received a text alert to warn me that I must restore the balance by midnight or I would start to incur fees. This hung over me despite praying for strategy and help. So, when I received a letter an hour later with yet more news that was difficult to absorb, I fought with a flood of emotions that bubbled up and threatened my ability to concentrate. I was tearful and in turmoil. My chest ached, and my eyes streamed at the slightest thought about the negative impact I seemed to have had upon a situation.

As much as I told myself it was feedback that may have an element of truth, I couldn't deal with the surge of emotion that was 'rocking my boat'. I couldn't dismiss the information as unfounded criticism, but I also recognised how I was allowing this compounding hit to trigger some very unhelpful catastrophic thinking, along the lines of 'Nobody understands me', 'I might as well give up trying to communicate' and 'I'll never get out of this debt until I'm too old to benefit'. Ugly and painful thoughts like this are deceptive and destructive, yet convincing in the moment.

So as soon as I had the opportunity that day to switch my physical context, I visited my peaceful gym for a jacuzzi and a vigorous swim. The value of exercise is well-known as a strategy for tackling anxiety and depression as it helps to release endorphins and serotonin or "happy hormones" (which I naturally lack anyway). I made a conscious decision to co-operate with a truth principle, whatever I believed or felt like doing at that moment.

Controlled Outbursts

What I was doing was sensing the accumulating pressure of the reservoir of water behind the top gates of the lock I had entered. Here is a picture of the need for calibration. If I had pushed those top gates with force, first it would have been difficult if not impossible to release the pressure as the weight of the water in the top reservoir resists the direction of the gate swinging. Not only this but the moment a fraction of space opened between these wooden gates, the height of the water column would burst through the seam causing severe turbulence, flooding and possible sinking of the bow of the vessel below.

Correct equilibrium is reached, instead, in a much less dramatic way (none of us appreciate drama queens, and this explains why they struggle to navigate life). First, by opening paddles in the lock wall of the higher body of water, and sometimes also within the gates themselves, we release the water pressure *under* the surface. The way I was taught to manage my own negative feelings as a young Christian was to follow the example of David and *'speak to my soul'*. Privately, deep within my soul, under the surface of visible emotionality, I am to lift the paddles or valves and allow calibration of soul with spirit.

Spirit mingles and refreshes the weary soul by its entrance by grace, through faith of the lifting of the paddles that allow in or out, the Water of Life. This happens by exercising co-operation of the soul through

- your *will*: the choice not to wallow and dramatise the threat of a breaking dam

- your *mind*: that knows what to do to escape this dangerous cycle

- and finally, your *emotions*: recognised, validated and processed to the benefit and growth and progress of your life, without becoming a spectacle themselves.

Picture 2: Controlled Calibration of the Soul

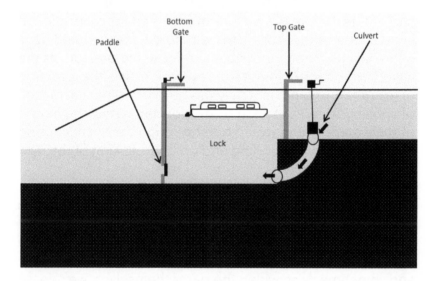

So, the ascent of the changing levels of the passing countryside in a narrowboat is a challenge. The narrowboat doesn't merely elevate, turn (except in designated places) leap or bend. Only the etiquette of the waterway can carry the vessel forward. Just a working knowledge and application of the lore of the canal will allow safe and efficient passage to its destination. No amount of fighting, pushing, crying, swearing or bargaining will have the slightest impact.

You and I must humble ourselves to the simple directions and designated practises.

Desires test us daily and we too must test them in return.

Should you exacerbate the fear, you are sunk.
Or should you deny the fear, you flunk it anyway by stagnating in a place of pretence and bravado, achieving nothing.

Trust is the great calibrator of emotion, the transformer of either desperate human force or even languid passivity. Both are harnessed for good when He receives our permission to direct the watercourse of our lives when our heart is given into His hands both to be weighed and tried

> "The King's heart is in the hand of the Lord, as are the watercourses; He turns it whichever way it wills. Every way of a man is right in his own eyes, but the Lord weighs and tries the hearts"
>
> (Proverbs 21:1-2)

Strong's Greek dictionary defines *kardía* or *heart* as 'the *affective* centre of our being'. It is the source of our desires and that which makes us who we are. You must acknowledge, experience and regulate your emotions without stifling them so that you can be sure of who you are in Him alone and so become a person of the highest stature.

What if you could trust your feelings to show your true desires?

What if those feelings betray doubt?

What if you deny the unwelcome doubts and push ahead, for better or for worse?

CHAPTER 5

WILLPOWER - WILL ANY DREAM DO?

Dripping wooden walls tower above me as I crane my neck to view the soaring height of the enclosure, its scale amplified in the parallel row of imposing poplars lining the banks. One or two passers-by peer down and haul their dogs back from the edge of the kerb. Showers of sandy dirt rattle onto my glasses, and I shake my head with irritation. It's a waiting game. Even with advice and encouragement nothing will speed up this afternoon's progress, and the flush of excitement for each batch of strollers happening upon the scene soon becomes a tiresome delay for all. Their only light relief is that one of their group is goaded into throwing a half-finished can of coke onto the deck. They run off before I can rustle up the energy to weakly chastise them.

Here I am a sitting duck, where is that lock keeper?

Being cut off from light and momentum; trapped within the tiny pool, I reflect upon my impossible predicament. Too committed to go back, too overwhelmed to go

forward and publicly stalled for the benefit of the curious, unsympathetic and amused I feel powerless to initiate any solution.

The Lock of Determination

One of the compliments my first husband paid me in his wedding reception speech was, *"she is a disciplined girl"*. In other words, he admired the fact that, though I could feel a pressing challenge, the emotions it prompted were not allowed to threaten my purposeful activity.

So far, I had considered the course before me, felt and denied the fear and chosen to relegate any intellectual or logical understanding of the destiny I sensed (perhaps as Jesus had, when he set his face like flint[1]). I steeled my resolve and launched the ship. Resolving to embrace the challenge of His predestined path, Jesus knew the cost was terrific. The difference was that He had counted the cost beforehand in a once and for all struggle with the will of His Father, on the eve of His crucifixion in the Garden of Gethsemane.

> *"Father, if you are willing, please take this cup of suffering away from me. Yet I want your will to be done, not mine"*

> (Luke, 22:42 NLT)

I too was hoping to achieve the will of my Father but glibly thought to beat a track by my own will through sheer determination. The wave after wave of relentless setbacks took their toll by repeatedly surprising me and wearing down my energy, month by month and year by year. I'm sure this was because I was not accessing the energy Paul lived so reliantly by, *"so powerfully at work within me"*.

I closed my eyes, drew back the curtain, to see for certain what I thought I knew

Things weren't working out too well.

As in the 'Joseph' lyrics of Andrew Lloyd-Webber's world-famous musical, I might have been tempted to ask, "Will any dream do?"[2]. Was the fact that I had a dream to pursue as significant as believing in a pre-destined and God-purposed reason for being?

Why was I so hung up on this course?

My motives were admirable at the outset, but hindsight teaches that 'the good' can be deceptively alluring. In my case, the effort for 'good' became the enemy of 'the best' God had intended for me and through me.

In fact, I didn't know what that 'best' looked like. Any other dream, anyone else's dream, was working out better than mine.

I comforted these ugly thoughts with the mantra, 'God sees; he knows my heart'.

Sacrifice and generosity are significant only if the source from which they are given can be replenished. I thought God expected that I should live in a costly manner, but such a lifestyle proved to be unsustainable because there wasn't a higher 'run-off' of favour replacing my sacrificial deposits. Now I understand that if He had blessed this mentality, He would have condemned me to continue to live in this distorted way.

Therefore, I urge you, brothers and sisters, by the mercies of God, to present your bodies [dedicating all of yourselves, set apart] as a living sacrifice, holy and well-pleasing to God, which is your rational (logical, intelligent) act of worship.

(Romans, 12:1)

Here Paul was saying that our sacrificial act of worship can and should be intelligently and rationally informed. He means that God is thrilled when we educate our spiritual act of sacrifice with a rational and logical contribution to the conversation. When we out-promise our capacity to give, we get into the dangerous waters of spiritual 'pay-day loans'. As in the natural order of financial crashes, spiritual interest rates can be extortionate and crippling.

I can point to some acts of worship I made that were presumptuous and emotively stirred. When I left my secure public service salaried position as a hospice nurse to pursue pastoral leadership and an uncertain financial funding award, I was not counting the cost. I was blindly exercising my own self-will to make God's purposes happen.

Floating on mud

This is the equivalent of trying to float a narrowboat on mud. A canal is a road paved with water. Water is the most perfect road surface. It is as even as a spirit-level, hardwearing and renewable. Just like the relationship we have with God through the Holy Spirit. It's buoyant, it eases and lubricates the friction of our daily travel and must be refreshed daily to prevent the risk of scraping the hull along the bottom or running aground.

Thank God, He cut the channel of our relationship with Him in advance. Water is tough to control. It will always find the point of least resistance and will only stand still if its bed is level. God has seen to the integrity of all that. The presence of the Holy Spirit is based upon an eternal and secure foundation of the love of the Father and the sacrifice of the Son. This is what will carry us safely and efficiently without loss or damage.

A reservoir that never runs dry

Water supply was one of the engineering challenges of the canal builders, especially in dry seasons of the year or during the passage of heavy traffic along the waterways. What a beautiful picture is this emptying of self - of the co-operation of the Trinity on our behalf and of our tri-part human co-operation with Him!

> *"no one can enter the kingdom of God unless they are born of water and the Spirit. Flesh gives birth to flesh, but the Spirit gives birth to spirit. You should not be surprised at my saying, 'You must be born again.' The wind blows wherever it pleases. You hear its sound, but you cannot tell where it comes from or where it is going. So, it is with everyone born of the spirit"*

> (John 3: 5-8, NIV)

Effort and willpower do not give birth to God's spiritual grace

Vain resolve to apply willpower can only ever give birth to more resolve to exercise even more willpower. The blessing and favour of God's spiritual life always gives birth to more spiritual life. The spiritual input to decisions may seem illusory, vulnerable and elusive like an invisible wind or a hard-to-trace leak but its impact is indisputable. Nowhere is this more obvious than when a season in life becomes more than usually challenging.

Take the challenge of ascending a hill via the waterway. Rivers do not climb hills, they only descend hills. That is what comes naturally to water. So, any canal descending a hillside only requires a small measure of water to navigate a series of descending locks. The top-lock, once entered, may then be emptied into a second lock. The water level in the second lock is raised to that of the first and the narrowboat sails into it. The water in the second lock is released into the third and the narrowboat sails into that too. Theoretically, this narrowboat can sail right down a flight of descending locks using the same approximate volume of one swimming pool's water repeatedly[3].

There is a measure of favour or spiritual grace for any ordinary day. However, in times of ascent, when no natural laws are working in your favour (of gravity in our case), you need multiple volumes of spiritual grace. Each lock in the flight requires a whole swimming pool full of water from the destination lock above. Each infilled lock is taken from that above it, which, to fill, takes another lock's contents from above it. And so on. Just as a canal lock is a hydraulic lift for the narrowboat, the grace of the Holy Spirit gives a spiritual lift to the life that demands anointing from above.

Picture 3. Descent of a three-rise lock

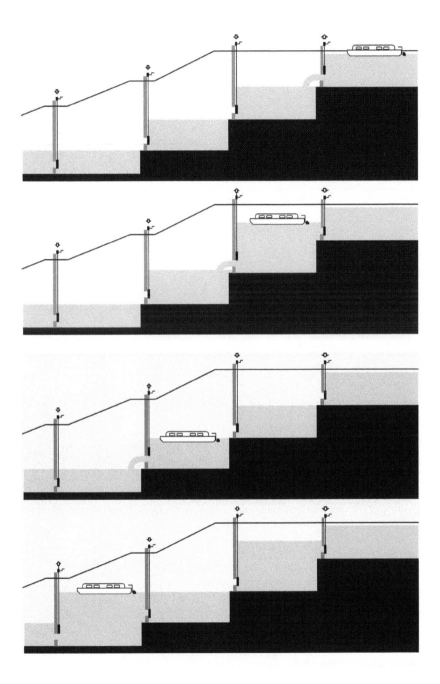

Picture 4. Ascent of a three-rise lock

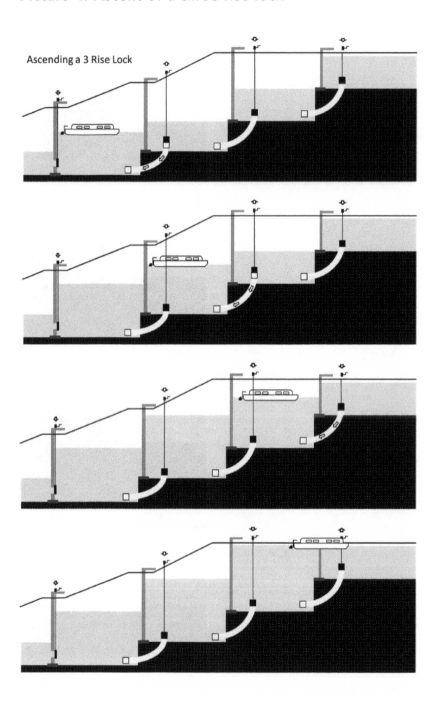

Ascending a 3 Rise Lock

Loss Leaders

In retail, a *'loss leader'* is an item that is sold below cost-price to stimulate other profitable sales. It is a profitable, though risky sales promotion technique. It's a risk that the larger supermarkets can afford to absorb.

Loss leaders are an essential part of companies' marketing and sales strategies offered to get the customer to part with more money than they intended. An example would be a supermarket selling sugar or milk at less than cost to draw customers to that supermarket chain.

Once in the store, they are likely to buy other goods. The loss incurred by the leader product is offset by the mark up on the additional items. It's a technique that makes sense, although risky. If it draws enough customers, the losses are more than offset.

Paul understood this, and he was the best example, after Christ, of a man who had counted the cost and deemed it worthwhile even if there should be no apparent return on the investment to him personally.

> But whatever was to my profit I now consider loss for the sake of Christ. What is more, I consider everything a loss compared to the surpassing greatness of knowing Christ Jesus my Lord, for whose sake I have lost all things. I consider them rubbish, that I may gain Christ...
>
> (Philippians 3:7-8, NIV)

Someone somewhere invested more time and money than they should have. I did. They've been the loss leader and their gifts are incredible if received with a response of gratitude.

However, there must come a day when loss leaders see to it that the customers are diversifying their tastes and are adding in other products from the shelves. A shop that sells only its loss leader products to bargain hunters will soon have to compensate by marking up everything else until the general brand becomes disproportionately expensive to the consumer.

Pearl before Swine

Expensive sacrifice in the context of the canal cruise is seen when a leader has poured themselves out like a lock emptying into an adjacent pool. When the secondary pool has insecure lock gates that leak or have been carelessly left open, this makes no sense. The original sacrifice is devalued, nothing is gained, and a clumsy effort to reclaim one's investment may even kick in.

God would rather that we learn from such mistakes, betrayals or even sabotage. This is what Jesus meant when he warned the generous-hearted not to throw their pearl before swine[4]. Is this not what Paul described as an extreme degree of service when he said,

> "it is God who is producing in you both the desire and the ability to do what pleases him...I will be proud when the Messiah returns that I did not run in vain or work hard in vain. Yet even if I am being poured out like an offering as part of the sacrifice and service I offer for your faith, I rejoice, and I share my joy with all of you. In the same way, you also should rejoice and share your joy with me."

(Philippians 2:13, 16-17, ISV)

Paul wanted to give his life for a purpose; a measurable and definitive meaning. Surely that is the case for most people.

However, I stray into the territory of the next sentiment or part of this book when I say he stated that "*Even If!*" his sacrifice was poured out in emptiness, and it seemed his life had been wasted for no reason, he would rejoice. Where I had run aground, Paul had even got past the "*What If?*" (*it doesn't happen*). He embraced and did not even perish the thought of failing!

I cannot say I am *at all* comfortable with the prospect of a life lived in vain. I do not believe God wants us to live a life in vain, or without impact. However, He greatly values our position of not insisting on experiencing the obvious results to know His approval.

Such trust turns into a life of unconditional conviction and certainty. Then great impact and fruitfulness can be released from it.

This comes from a broken will; broken in the sense that it has bowed to a new master - not reason, not emotion, not self-will but to the spirit.

Relief and peace

Paul Scanlon, founder of Life Church, UK[5] once said "*What you have to work hard to get, you will have to work hard to keep*". How true a test this is of anything one is tempted to say "*God told me to...*"

When I laid down my career for a calling, even against certain reasoning and personal emotional caution, I found that I took my striving straight into church life. There was no relief. I continued fighting to maintain any semblance of confidence and composure within my chosen world.

If she had still been present in my life, my late pastor Lil would have reminded me then of the concept of 'will worship'[6.] To elevate the power of decision over and above the conviction of the Holy Spirit (whether it be an assuring whisper heard or imagined) is dangerous. This is to trust in one's own ability to follow through upon principle rather than dependence. Will worship is a form of idolatry that elevates human intention and self-determination above the leading of an unfolding dialogue between God and man.

Making wise, godly decisions is a vital and God-given ability but deciding something and leading from decision rather than conviction can be a trap. Sheer grit and determination soon becomes a frustrating journey. You can see we are on common ground with this human weakness when you read that the great apostle Paul was also familiar with this trap.

> I do not understand my own actions. For I do not do what I want, but I do the very thing I hate. Now if I do what I do not want, I agree with the law, that it is good. So now it is no longer I who do it, but sin that dwells within me. For I know that nothing good dwells in me, that is, in my flesh. For I have the desire to do what is right, but not the ability to carry it out. For I do not do the good I want, but the evil I do not want is what I keep on doing.

(Romans 7:15-19, ESV).

Paul led us artfully to the point that on our own we can do nothing of value. The only way for the Christian is to walk 'after the spirit' and not the flesh, to be 'spiritually' and not 'carnally minded'. The two are in conflict, and the only answer to the nagging doubt 'What if?' is to pray.

To pray is to acknowledge that your power is finite, your knowledge is probably corrupted, and it declares that your emotions are not your master.

Worldwide Hillsong church planter and leader Bobbie Houston in her 20th anniversary year of "Colour Conference" made a statement at Colour in London, 2016[7], acknowledging there is no way such a movement could have happened but by the hand of God, she beautifully summarised the antidote to the obstructions, the lessons of *As If* so far.

"Let prayer do the work"

PROSTRATION (OR FALLING) BRIDGE

YOU SHOUT, "IF ONLY!"

Jacob looked up and there was Esau, coming with his four hundred men; so he divided the children among Leah, Rachel and the two female servants. 2 He put the female servants and their children in front, Leah and her children next, and Rachel and Joseph in the rear. 3 He himself went on ahead and bowed down to the ground seven times as he approached his brother.

4 But Esau ran to meet Jacob and embraced him; he threw his arms around his neck and kissed him. And they wept. 5 Then Esau looked up and saw the women and children. "Who are these with you?" he asked.

Jacob answered, "They are the children God has graciously given your servant."

6 Then the female servants and their children approached and bowed down. 7 Next, Leah and her children came and bowed down. Last of all came Joseph and Rachel, and they too bowed down.

8 Esau asked, "What's the meaning of all these flocks and herds I met?"

"To find favor in your eyes, my lord," he said.

9 But Esau said, "I already have plenty, my brother. Keep what you have for yourself."

10 "No, please!" said Jacob. "If I have found favor in your eyes, accept this gift from me. For to see your face is like seeing the face of God, now that you have received me favorably. 11 Please accept the present that was brought to you, for God has been gracious to me and I have all I need." And because Jacob insisted, Esau accepted it.

(Genesis 33:1-11, NIV)

If only I had watched her

I was aching and tired, ready for a cup of tea as the earlier ice-cream had made me quite thirsty. Trea had been glum since she dropped Dragon into the canal. Certainly, the shine had worn off our day trip and we needed to head home.

But, where was she?

Trea had slipped from my side and was nowhere to be seen. The light was grey, and the colours of her patterned dress had leached in the twilight, making it easy for her to hide. I knew that her little game was merely that, an innocent game meant to entertain herself as she saw my escalating confusion.

It was a few minutes before a small crowd of day-trippers had rallied to my assistance to comfort and assure me that she would be close at hand and easy to find. I was weak with anxiety. She would not realise the stress she was putting me through. Maybe she even found it amusing to think of the stir she had caused.

However, I was wrong. She had squeezed into a narrow space between a buried piece of vertical corrugated iron and a boatshed. Realising her backfiring joke, she was experiencing the terrific dilemma of needing to own up.

'If only I could get out of this' Trea thought. 'If only I hadn't done it'.

It was inevitable she was the offender and would be in serious trouble.

My newly-formed search crew drew close to the canal itself, looking behind tree trunks and peering up into the branches. They had seated me with my back to them, protectively circled by a few thoughtful families. Their men played torchlights on the quayside steps and reflecting water. These were stifling, dread-filled moments where no words could appease me and only the gentle touch and presence of my fellow companions offered a degree of awkward solace.

Then Trea scrabbled out of her inhospitable niche, as anxiety about spiders got the better of her. She approached the semi-circle of women on the bank, crying and anticipating an outburst of anger and blame.

Instead, she was gathered up with a swoop of joy and exclamation. She was aware that she should have been disciplined, but all I could do was hug her tightly and with thanksgiving. She was puzzled. At the extreme of her own thoughtlessness and nonsense, she was being lavished with love and relief.

Evidently, she mattered more than my need to point out the error of her ways.

We were both humbled by this episode as we recognised, in our own ways, a new understanding of the priority of precious relationship rather than correction.

CHAPTER 6
MIND THE GAP!

For a stretch of uninterrupted meandering, the narrowboat lazily swallows the short distance between two locks. An occasional vessel passes, arousing in me, thoughts about where the passengers have come from and whether they will find the destination they are looking for. When I arrive at the foot of the five-rise, I will be dwarfed by the height of the weighty lock gates. Here my grasp of navigational principles will be put to the test, costing me time, effort and humbling adjustments to my premature sense of mastery. I recognise how much I have forgotten already since setting out. I feel unprepared for the locks and wonder how my companion can so comfortably handle the vessel without acknowledging his inexperience or the demands of the coming days. Perhaps no one will be there to help us, or the mechanism will have rusted?

I retire without sleeping, irritated by the slapping of wavelets against the hull. Stirring again, I emerge into the total darkness of the night, rustling oaks taunting and

applauding each dire suggestion projecting distortedly onto my weary mental screen. Waking from a fitful sleep I see that scenery has started to change as the waterway opens out into a basin cradling the five-tiered grandiosity ahead.

The pound between rises

I spent five years straining toward a perceived destiny and a further two, painfully losing my grip on what I thought would take me there. My strength and hope and joy and peace were slipping away alarmingly. My soul's mind, heart and will became the focus of circumstantial assault upon the God-given facts. I was typical of thousands who have missed the path of peace by fixing my eyes on anything I had to do other than Jesus, for whom I was doing all this stuff!

Composed of three elements, the soul's lifework is to submit its mind, emotions, and will to God to become Spirit-led rather than self-sufficient. You lay down the mental demand for understanding. You put away the tendency to lean upon your own willpower to make it happen or rely upon emotional stability. All this is the fickleness of self-sufficiency.

To submit all three; mind, emotion, and will to what God says, He asks that in faith you see yourself at the end of your journey. All you must submit to - is *His* say so. See your narrowboat at its destination, not somewhere else. He enables you in your preparation as the Bride of Christ, the church. He prepares you for your long-expected day of consummation. The Bible calls this the *consummation of your faith, the salvation of your souls.*

> *You are, "receiving as the result the outcome, the consummation of your faith, the salvation of your souls"*

> (1 Peter, 1:9)

This is the mysterious union of your call and destiny

Where once there was doubt, disconnection, and massive contradiction, now settles integrity, wholehearted assurance, and solid, tangible faith. Peace, stillness, no sense of hurry but confident expectation.

What does this consummation of faith mean? In that intimate place of surrender, you find that even if the world has gone dark, the light that seemed to disappear like the setting sun, will arise again as certainly as the new day will come.

God says that you can do better than looking back with hindsight, *only then* agreeing with Him. You can see in advance that you are blessed. You can see with foresight, with the foresight of faith.

> *"Then they asked him, "What must we do to do the works God requires?" Jesus answered, "The work of God is this: to believe in the one he has sent"*

> (John 6:28-29, NIV)

Speaking out what He says you are and what you are here for confirms and seals your faith.

> *".......if you confess with your mouth, "Jesus is Lord," and believe in your heart that God raised him from the dead, you will be saved. For it is with your heart that you believe and are justified, and it is with your mouth that you confess and are saved"*

> (Romans 10:9-10, NIV)

Faith fills the gap between call and destiny.

It is the belief that you will eventually look back upon a blessing that is yet to come. Someone once explained that vision is the picture postcard sent to you from the future.

Faith believes that you will live there one day!

Halfway along the canal in the gathering gloom, you realise that *you* could even be the obstacle between your own call and destiny. In believing, God dissolves you, yes, your very self. His anointing flows into and oils your mind, will, and emotions and sanctifies them for the thing He sees from completion. This brings faith to completion and unifies you with your destiny. Now, even in utter darkness, you see where you are going.

Have you ever been at the point that you cried?
"God show me your ways?"
Or, *"Come through or I'm through!"*
God loves that kind of desperation and desire.

I've spent time at the altar when I've been convinced of an imminent visitation by God Himself, a brush of the hem of his garment, or a whisper in my ear. At times I've felt as if I've tiptoed on the edge of heaven. I've also got up deflated and disappointed from many of those intense appeals (and then feared to allow myself into that place of extremity and risk ever again).

On repeated occasions and sometimes for months at a time there was a physical pain in my heart as my spirit cried out for the purposes of God to be fulfilled in my life as well as in the wider Body of Christ. I knew His Kingdom *is* coming, but how and when?

> *"Jesus, grilled by the Pharisees on when the kingdom of God would come, answered, "The kingdom of God doesn't come by counting the days on the calendar. Nor when someone says, 'Look here!' or, 'There it is!' And why? Because God's kingdom is already among you."*

He went on to say to his disciples, "The days are coming when you are going to be desperately homesick for just a glimpse of one of the days of the Son of Man, and you won't see a thing. And they'll say to you, 'Look over there!' or, 'Look here!' Don't fall for any of that nonsense. The arrival of the Son of Man is not something you go out to see. He simply comes.

"You know how the whole sky lights up from a single flash of lightning? That's how it will be on the Day of the Son of Man. But first, it's necessary that he suffer many things and be turned down by the people of today."

(Luke 17:20-25, The Message)

"Are we there yet?"

"Why is there a difference between what God is doing here in my world and out there?" I once asked. There was such a yawning gap. Could this gathering sense of urgency, momentum, and pace be a sign of the time approaching when all things will be gathered up unto Him?[1].

Struggling with feelings of frustration, I recognised I had some developing to do and maturity to attain to. However, I also believed that it was right and possible to grow up fast. I read the gospels to align myself with the fresh enthusiasm and momentum that the disciples felt in their time. After Jesus ascended, there was such a sense that they would not be long waiting for the Last Day that two angels had had to come and tell them to stop looking up into the sky[2].

Jesus wants us to live daily in the keen expectation of His return, not to go to bed each night with a resigned 'Oh well, tomorrow's another day' but a real certainty that it will be, and that we ought to be ready for anything. I wanted to capture that readiness and expectancy in my life, to think that Jesus' disarming and yet accepting gaze could fall on me in any situation, bringing all at once, love, repentance, and abandonment into my life.

For me, however, layers of heartache, disappointment, and misunderstandings brought a heaviness and pain to the work of ministry to the point of near exhaustion and incredulity. Even the staunchest cheerleaders felt doubt about the credibility of continuing. These pressures built up in my spirit over my formative years. Together they made for intolerable tension between *what was* and what *was not yet*.

Hybels described this in *Courageous Leadership*[3], as the tension he felt halfway down a treacherous incline. He wrestled between daring to stay on a makeshift, brakeless go-kart and the inevitable injury of throwing himself off *now* rather than risking a more spectacular crash *later*.

In the face of every new offence to my faith, counter-attacks upon the validity of my stance would pile into my mind. Every single inspired contribution to the corporate sense of momentum and expectancy was ferociously attacked and timings snared.

Doubtful Grasping

Have you seen a demonstration of someone holding a chair first close to their body and then at arms-length? Soon the chair held at arms-length becomes heavy. The strain of a load held at a distance causes inefficiency, discomfort and exhaustion. The security of a load held in proximity ensures endurance and effectiveness.

This also happens when you perceive there to be a gap between where you are and where you want to be. Surely this is the story of the Christian walk. You strain forward to reach the goal; you try to close the gap between 'now and then'. That is the secret of success and fruitfulness, to keep moving toward the clear goal in sight with the means to cover the ground between.

You may ask....

What is the difference between where I am and where God would have me?

How can I close that gap, prevent the waste, delay and exhaustion?

What does it mean to press earnestly toward my goal?
Should I evaluate the risk of becoming disillusioned that it will never happen for me?
Won't I need another 25 years?
Why does that faze me?
Why should it be necessary for me to succeed *and fast*?
Why does it matter that I do not fail?

God desires that you should not have to learn all the same painful lessons first-hand. If only the children of Israel had realised that they had a choice between two weeks or forty years in the wilderness perhaps they would have chosen the shorter route. They would have found out it was also the quickest route. You too have the same kind of choices, and you will experience the same consequences of those choices.

What then is this *Gap*?

The Pocket Oxford Dictionary[4] describes 'gap' as

"a breach, empty space, interval, deficiency, wide divergence in views".

Travelling on the London Underground, one hears the phrase,

"Mind the Gap!"

It is a warning that seeks to protect ignorant or careless travellers from falling or dropping something into the space between the tube train and the platform. Either act would spell disaster for the person concerned. They might suffer loss of life or property, serious injury and at the very least, delay in the tube's departure *with consequences upon the time-tabling of the whole network of neighbouring and consequent trains.*

Tourists and newcomers tread gingerly over the edge of the platform, seasoned commuters are more carefree, (careless but confident) through habitual exposure to risk. Visitors hesitate, turn back to assist their children or friends, Londoners move on, the crowd moving almost as one, already gone from view before you have gathered up your pushchair and souvenirs. Could this be a picture of your life? You may travel clumsily or effortlessly, either because of familiarity or unfamiliarity with the patterns of the day. What more accurate picture of chaotic life could there be than a scene in a London Underground station at rush hour?

And yet, there is a pattern and a purpose to all of it.

Original Purpose

God created you to rule and reign, to have dominion over the earth and to be fruitful and multiply[5]. He calls you to confidence and familiarity, to surefootedness and elegance amongst the race of life. You have been given everything you need and yet can become distanced from it, fearful and unsure of who you are.

"His divine power has given us everything we need for life and godliness through our knowledge of Him who called us by his own glory and goodness. Through these, he has given us his very great and precious promises, so that through them you may participate in the divine nature and escape the corruption in the world caused by evil desires. For this very reason, make every effort to add to your faith, goodness; and to goodness knowledge; and to knowledge, self-control; and to self-control, perseverance; and to perseverance, godliness; and to godliness, brotherly kindness and to brotherly kindness, love. For if you possess these qualities in increasing measure, they will keep you from being ineffective and unproductive in your knowledge of our Lord Jesus Christ."

(2 Peter 1: 3-8, NIV)

You fall for the lie that you are insignificant either as an individual or as a local church. You watch bemused as others rush on by, travelling light, with their earplugs and mobile phones while you fight on the platform with your shopping bags and rucksack. You discount what you see and exclude yourself from countless possibilities because they are so unfamiliar, seemingly unattainable. But you are called to be people of a different spirit who know you are created for such a time as this. Recognise that the world will not stop for you and enjoy the ride. Living dangerously (you couldn't think anything else of life with Jesus) is the way it is to be. Otherwise, you will watch ineffectually while you become increasingly irrelevant.

Closing the gap

This is how the disciples were closing the gap - by living in the immediacy of God's presence and power. Are you creating gaps and interruptions in the flow of life where there should be continuity?

Do you prise open gaps that were never meant to be there?

- between your destination and your terminus

- between the theory and your practice

- between what Adam was intended to be and the entrance of sin[6]

- Between accepting Christ's sacrifice for sin and the commission to serve

- between He who is our source and the blessing He would love us to become[7]

- between your future and your present experience

    "that you can know and understand the hope to which He has called you and how rich is His glorious inheritance in the saints"

    (Ephesians 1:18-19)

- between your knowledge and your faith

    "Show me your faith without deeds"

    (James 2:18, NIV).

- between what Christ suffered for you and that which was lacking in His death? (The space in which we fulfil the challenge now left us by Christ's death and resurrection.

    "I fill up in my body what is still lacking in regard to Christ's afflictions, for the sake of his body, which is the church"

    (Colossians 1:24, NIV)

- between your intention and your activity

  "Let your "Yes" be Yes"

  (James 5:12, NIV)

Communion and intimacy

The link between communion and intimacy with God and the resultant effectiveness and authority of man was once marred forever. The distance between God and man, depicted by Michelangelo in the famous painting 'Creation of man' is merely an electrically charged hairs' breadth, but it became an unbridgeable divide.

God in the Old Testament was depicted as a just and holy God who was feared and only approachable in strictly defined conditions on pain of certain death if the priest should get it wrong. Man had to appease a holy God. If he dared, he might even wrestle with God[8]. The pattern went like this.

- Man followed laws that revealed his inadequacies
- Man waited with bated breath to see if God would accept his mean efforts
- If God should answer favourably, he was relieved.

But now, because of Jesus, separation of God's purpose from his people was resolved.

The **G-A-P** was sealed.

The G.A.P. is a vacuum inviting God's Awesome Power

Do you experience God and then follow this with dull intervening weeks? Do you have conversations with Christian friends that inspire and then are quickly forgotten? Do you enter worship that stirs you and then cannot be refreshed for another six weeks? Do you respond to altar calls that bring resolve until there is a practical application required from you? Is this your image of Christianity, full of erratic high points and gaps between?

His purpose IS his people, one and the same. And as you grow, His Kingdom is extended. You move beyond the tit for tat, linear, immature and time-bound exchanges and activity-dependent upon others. You grow organically and exponentially. Now your relationship with Him can be expansive, continual, internal and personal. You are 'in Him'[9] not merely 'waiting for Him' or for a sign or a word to grow older or wiser.

Life is imparted when you recognise these gaps and holes, where you admit there is discontinuity and delay. The separation of God's people from His purpose can now be re-connected and consummated.

"Where are you?"

God's question to Adam in the Garden on the day Adam realised the full implications of His disobedience was "Where are you?" To move Adam anywhere near relationship with God again, God had to make Adam realise the enormity of the gap between him and God. It was Adam who had distanced himself, and it is Adam in you distancing yourself from God. It is Adam in you trying to bridge the gap with your efforts to please Him, with your fig leaf coverings of self-effort, wisdom and good works.

You can stay where you are or come out and acknowledge that He alone can stem the breach in your life of sin and self, fear, hopelessness and uncertainty in an unstable world. Some of you go on hiding in a futile effort to save your life from shame and exposure. Sometimes you almost 'come out' and then shrink back[10]. But God only asks you to realise, you alone cannot do it, cannot run your life with success, cannot be the church successful, cannot afford to wait until you are better at 'it' before you launch out into deeper waters.

Spiritual Hydraulics

Remember GAP = God's awesome power!

This is the gap between the depth of water in one lock above the next. As the pressure of the water column in the higher body of water exceeds the lower, there sits a principle of potential power that may be harnessed either for deliverance or for disaster.

> "We are in a spiritual battle over our lives, our effectiveness, over our destinies and our city".

Here, George W. Bush, the 43rd President of the United States was speaking of the war against terrorism in the wake of the September 11th, 2001 World Trade Centre bombings by Al Qaeda. He went on, describing this new level of threat as a battle "without battlefields or beachheads"[11], against an invisible, dispersed and crippling enemy.

Do you long to know God? God rushes toward those who press into Him. Sometimes we come so close and yet remain so far apart; afraid that we may die without a breakthrough. The disciples on the road to Emmaus, almost missed it when Jesus acted as if he were going further without them[12]. The people who piled into boats to close the gap between themselves and Jesus on the other side of the lake were after his miracles rather than Himself[13].

Where will He come?

He will come and fill any gap you invite Him to reveal. Invite Him to bring conviction to the offending breaches as an inner tube puncture might be tested in a bucket of water.

The Kingdom will come as it will and should do, at its appointed time. By the instruction of the lock keeper, this can be quite sudden. The King will come in where He is invited, into those places where there is death to self (or your soul). This is an ancient and modern practice of repentance

Unobtrusively, it might seem random. In fact, it only ever happens because of secret preparation. *THAT'S* where the action will be. This is the restorative work of forgiveness. You see, the gap may only be tiny, even invisible, but until you ask Him to lock those gates, you allow the power of the purposes of God to leak, instead of accumulating.

And now your life is ready to carry weight, transmit power. It can respond to and convey authority.

CHAPTER 7
TOUCHING THE VOID

The lock-keepers along the Leeds-Liverpool canal go home at nightfall. There is no passage through the locks after dark. Not without grave danger or damage. Canal cruisers account for these enforced breaks, enjoying a quiet drink and a towpath barbeque without fretting about lost time or opportunity. They know that the new day and next leg of the journey will wait for the lock-keeper's guidance or at least the natural daylight they need. They are enjoying their cruise as much as they anticipate their destination. They epitomise the waterway motto that goes like this. *"To go fast, go slow"*

Coming to midway in my life journey the winds changed, skies lowered, and the light was failing fast. I had made some of that worse for myself by not mooring often enough to eat, rest and call it a day. I could have resumed the cruise later from this point, in fair weather. But what was rest? How could that be part of any progressive plan?

Ahead was gloom, intimidating featureless boughs scraped the hull, invisible liquid slapped as the wind whipped the channelled water. Strange swishes and the ominous screeches of anonymous wildlife started me with regularity. This would be a battle of nerves. Chugging engine noises granted familiar comfort even though I had dropped speed. In fact, the engine 'fitted' temperamentally and then cut out in a gravel-like slide into silence. The narrowboat floated on as I took in the fact that the tank was empty.

This was silence, a nerve-wracking chaos of imaginations, isolation, sickening fear and a conviction that something damaging had occurred under the surface. I couldn't stop now because I couldn't see where to align the boat, how to avoid veering into the jetty.

The Empty Lock

Next thing I knew, I fell right into 'The Gap'

> *"Jesus answered, "Are there not twelve hours of daylight? A man who walks by day will not stumble, for he sees by this world's light. It is when he walks by night that he stumbles, for he has no light."*

> (John 11:9-10, NIV)

I steeled myself for a long night

Many of your finest moments are borne from pressure, struggle, and resistance.

They say that the darkest hour is before the dawn. Inexplicable darkness setting in on the sunset of a bright success eats up the powerful and colourful sustaining vision of the world. In the face of the coming transient, dark night of the soul you can reassure yourselves of another inevitable cycle of light repeating itself.

Tomorrow will come.

There is something refreshing and hopeful about the emerging dawn of a new day. It can bring relief, herald significance or merely remind your diurnal nature to kick-start again. Here is the threshold of another beginning, renewed application or new insight. Even sudden understanding and perspective may come tomorrow.

Prostrated

One day early in January 2006, during my first week of leaving all secular employment, I took a blank desk-pad and mapped out the insights from the previous two years of journaling. Finally, I had left work for a ministry as a Pastor. After holding the improbable dream of working in church ministry for over six years, I was lying on the lounge carpet this winter Monday morning, dedicating time to review the previous leg of the journey and to pray for the future changes ahead. The gas fire 'put-putted' comfortingly, but I was intent on progress. I had no idea how, but I was not going to have any regrets, I was free.
I was desperate to do life differently!

I was reading the chronological account of Jacob's stop-start journey. I saw clearly for the first time in awful reality, my view of God was as distant and impartial, an observer who was unreachable. The fact Jesus had spanned the divide between us had only informed my mind and did not seem to have touched my heart. It was a crucial discovery of my journey that although I had a saving relationship with God, and I was on an inevitable route to eternity, I had no regular living impact of that fact within my experience. My desire now was to close the gap I mentioned earlier.

"to know Christ and the power of his resurrection and the fellowship of sharing in his sufferings, becoming like him in his death"

(Philippians 3:10, NIV)

These Scriptures were precious gifts whose recent arrival in my life had all the power to change me in this way, but it was to be some time before their potential was fulfilled.

"For it is by grace you have been saved, through faith — and this not from yourselves, it is the gift of God — not by works, so that no-one can boast"

(Ephesians 2:8-9, NIV)

How could I think otherwise?

I never doubted the truth that Jesus took upon himself the crushing burdens of the world in his acceptance of a horrific death on the cross. Yet artistic and sensitive souls as I, are prone to becoming burdened by the pain and woes of the world.

You and I must grasp that we are entirely unable to pour ourselves out in any significant way other than by lifting His name as thanks for His sacrifice. It is a matter of allowing any burden to remain as His burden and not ours. He shed blood so that we would not need to. Our sacrifice to him need not be a bloody one again because He was perfect and acceptable to God once and for all.

Have you understood the difference between law and grace? It is a factual truth - Jesus' death was a substitution for the redeeming price of the penalty fee we owed God.

I did not live as though I had grasped this.

Neither did I see that Bible character after character lived their lives out in unedited imperfection and glory to illustrate principles so that I might save myself some trouble. Even before Jesus came as a man, God was trying to get us to understand the gulf between us. When he said that Abel's sacrifice of meat to God was acceptable to Him, it was not because it was *meat* but because Abel believed the meat was *acceptable*. It was not the animal's bloodshed that made Abel's sacrifice acceptable to God, rather how much Abel believed in its power.

Jesus' blood was poured out for you.

Only your belief in its power, not the blood itself, will redeem your paltry efforts.

One of the most continuous challenges in your walk is that your faith should have more effect on your perceptions about life and its direction or flow than your circumstances do.

A Broken life is a blessed life

Jacob was acquainted with the power of circumstances in testing and transforming his capacity to believe God. Jacob demonstrated brokenness as the medium for blessing, and you must be ready for this discipline too. There is a paradox that as Jacob became more broken, he became more useful and effective (like a schooled horse having learned its master's codes of communication).

Similarly, as a pot or receptacle becomes broken, it may no longer hold the measured volume of water poured in. Now it becomes a more visible distributor of life flow. Cracked and leaking, it adds diversion and display rather than being efficient. The pot almost becomes irrelevant as a container. Its purpose is no longer to contain but to exaggerate, adding noise, attraction, movement, and range to its display.

God loves to work like this with us. He even chooses to need us although He could do it Himself. The brokenness He requires is not the destruction of a person's make-up. It is the conquering of the soul; their mind, will and emotions. Remember, the salvation of the soul is the consummation of your faith? And as each of you submit your own interpretations of what you think you should *do* about your circumstances, as you submit them to what He would do about them, you are strengthened and not weakened.

To refer to someone as 'broken' is an expression of alarm at the state of someone who was once great or influential or respected. Perhaps they are alcoholic, deserted by their spouse, widowed or imprisoned, spent upon a great work or initiative that has drained them dry. Their situation has shattered their thinking and emotions and their outlook is altered. Within a Christian context, the word 'broken' may describe a submitted life. Many misunderstand such a meaning of brokenness as *'done for'*, damaged or irreparably altered.

Some looked upon Mary Magdalene as broken in this way.

> *"When a woman who had lived a sinful life in that town learned that Jesus was eating at the Pharisee's house, she brought an alabaster jar of perfume, and as she stood behind him at his feet weeping, she began to wet his feet with her tears. Then she wiped them with her hair, kissed them and poured perfume on them,"*

> (Luke 7:37-38, NIV)

The woman with the alabaster jar was a broken person as far as the world was concerned. She was a prostitute, a reject in society. She knew her need of God and was abandoned in her worship of God. She knew she could not pour out any sacrifice large enough to honour Him. She simply stayed at

Jesus' feet. Her adoration was the reason she was exalted rather than the broken box of perfume she gave him.

She points you to the fact that the call upon believers today is not to be cloistered within the familiar containment of safe church life. And gathering together, you may move into the neighbourhood, outside the church wall where His blood was shed, for the sake of the many who do not know him. Your brokenness is demonstrated by the character of Christ which is to seek and to serve the lost and the hurting and the broken. It's a different brokenness to the wearing out and breaking down of bitter life experiences. It is not necessarily a brokenness that has been arrived at through a wasted life of disappointment and hardship.

Yet marvellously, even this is an acceptable offering when it is relinquished to Him.

Didn't I say that brokenness is a sacrificial response to Christ with no more shedding of blood? Don't we long for our children not to have to learn the hard way? A broken will doesn't have to be a grand finale after five years' battling with parents, experimenting with drugs or seeing one's peers depressed or taking their own lives.

There is a softer route of brokenness. A believing submission to God's right choices and direction is the happiest way to learn and grow. It is a sweet aroma to God to see this kind of pure and expensive sacrificial living being poured out in His name and for His purpose. We are no longer bleeding but praising living sacrifices, flowing into the streets and houses outside our private lives or local church walls[1].

Perfect lives

Some say that brokenness cannot be the will of God because He died to make us whole and He was broken so we could be mended. Then there is never any justification for us to be less than intact. Your resulting lives would be perfect and sinless, healthy, perfected and whole. Your lives would be smooth, sculpted alabaster jars, beautiful to look at and to touch, full of perfume to gloat about. If this is the doctrine you live by, where does that leave you if your cold turns to flu if your teenager is rebelling and the doctor suggests you need antidepressants?

There is only one conclusion, either you or God, have failed. You will fail. In fact, if you stay intact, it's probably because you are made of plastic rather than the fragile clay vessels of the apostle Paul likens us to.

> *"But we have this treasure in jars of clay to show that this all-surpassing power is from God and not from us. We are hard pressed on every side, but not crushed; perplexed, but not in despair; persecuted, but not abandoned; struck down, but not destroyed. We always carry around in our body the death of Jesus, so that the life of Jesus may also be revealed in our body,"*

> (2 Corinthians 4:7-10, NIV)

If you stay 'intact' then how does the perfume of your life flow from it? If God is God, then it is you who fail. But there is no need for condemnation anymore. Do not forget that the gospel is and always will be a gospel for a people who fail yet become great in the realisation of that failure.

Paul said, *"when I am weak then I am strong!"* Pretending there are never any problems and never any setbacks will keep you guilty and defeated as a failure. But they are God's problems and God's setbacks and given to Him can become God's glory in you. You must become free in the face of your weaknesses, to interpret them not as weaknesses but as opportunities for God's strength to shine through and flow from you. If you cling on to your doctrine of perfection, if you keep the lid shut on your private supply of life you can never raise your head above the church walls where you are faced with the challenges of your own imperfections and inadequacies. Let's be honest - this happens IN the church as well as beyond it.

People watch to see what you do under pressure. They want to know that the flow continues, and the life-source is still there for them to partake of. After building relationships and letting people see into your life, they need to know that your first response is not to defend and protect self-interest as Jacob did at first.

I trust in You

Mary's alabaster jar held something precious, but only until it was needed.

Then it had to be broken.
You, too, are effective only when sacrificially and liberally poured out.

In the right moment.
Your defining moment.

Mary's pure nard (her defining moment) was so valuable that the onlookers said she should have used it sparingly, done what she could first and then had more for a rainy day. Now she was in the position of not knowing where her next portion might come from. She was dependent upon God. When you love Him, worship Him, serve in the House and despite personal needs and personal imperfections, give away what you can, then, when such sacrifice is the norm, God delights to honour and to mark you out as significant in your time[2].

Only He can do that.

Brokenness is entirely scriptural though God does not dictate bad circumstances to cause this to happen. Brokenness is a response you can increasingly choose to make at the lightest touch of God's favour, presence or discipline. His work in you and through leadership of you and by you is to help you to learn to respond sensitively and easily (without such a fight as I had) before being convinced He knows best.

I hope you learn faster than me.

Brokenness can come without fighting first. That would be the kind of brokenness that doesn't wait to be in the gutter where there is nothing to lose. Indeed, why not submit while you have everything to lose? God would prefer that you submit to His hand upon you without the need of painful lessons.

I have found, despite the appearance of evil, the reverse is true. As you lose your life, you find it. The Christian life is a journey of increasing brokenness. As you are broken, you are made whole. Yet even in the depths of pain and shattered life, some people are still not broken. Even the persecuted martyrs and the prophetic Hoseas and Jeremiahs amongst us must realise that *difficulty does not have any redeeming benefit.*

You must still choose to be whole because of brokenness.

As a hospice nurse, I saw just about every possible reaction to cancer that there could be. Cancer itself is not the killer, it is the response to it that takes the life of the person away or redeems the person's ability to live within the time they have. *Whether being broken by life is God's will or the devil's is not the point. Brokenness is a quality that we can arrive at the easy or the hard way.*

Either way, it is a spiritual quality loved and attractive to God.

Touching the Void

I call this brokenness paradox, Touching the Void.

In 1985, an incredible account of survival unfolded[3]. Two mountaineers tackled the unclimbed west face of the fearsome 21,000ft Siula Grande in the Peruvian Andes. Having slipped on a ledge, Joe Simpson hung precariously over a crevasse. His companion Simon faced the agonising decision to cut the rope by which he too was being pulled by Joe's weight, into oblivion. Choosing the lesser of two evils, he cut the lifeline of his trusted companion to prevent two certain deaths. Joe shrieked as the rope was severed. Plummeting into the yawning belly of the mountain he fell beyond sight and sound, beyond help and even hope.

Joe fell into the crevasse, miraculously awaking in bewilderment some unmeasured time later upon a tiny ledge that had interrupted what should have been an inevitably fatal fall.

He was alive - gravely injured, mangled. In acute pain *and alive*. The miracle of this save wore thin over the ensuing hours and hours in which Joe realised he was lost anyway, victim to a slow and agonising lapse into dehydrated unconsciousness. Instead, he chose to die quickly. Terrified, he gave himself up into the jaws of the crevasse, shouting as he rolled off the ledge and fell deeper still again to certain death.

Incredibly, he woke up again on an internal packed snow ramp along which he crept upward, toward a deep exit onto the face of mountain snowfields he had traversed days earlier.

So, you, too, may dare to abandon yourself in the face of the yawning and awful emptiness of self-limitation. You touch the void of your total lost-ness and inability where gratitude and intimate desire for Him wells up.

But you are not to wallow in that void once you have touched it. Watchman Nee, the great Chinese theologian who suffered twenty years in solitude and confinement for his faith, wrote that the spirit of trust is essential to prayer[4]. Suddenly, prayer becomes one's vital breath and hope rather than an obligatory guilt-ridden exercise. It is now located in the intimacy and availability and power of God to lift you from what and where you are. Locating the way of escape is now an absolute urgency for you and for those who need to hear about this submissive encounter.

What depth of deficiency will it take to teach you who you are in God?

His Word and his Voice through the church speaks into your life. As an unbelieving believer, do you believe in God but not His word? Do you insist upon waiting for the third voice of circumstance?

Dare to go with that thought, to the fear deep within you and be brought face to face with your own inadequacies. You can admit that your life is in the clutch of inevitable death. There you are trapped and caught within a grave beyond rescue.

Too damaged to climb out: too weak to hold on.
Frightened, you might descend deeper into a habit, a lifestyle, a relationship or ill health. Not knowing how to climb out of that hole, terrified of being separated from the reality you dream of.

Remember that *'hope deferred makes your heart sick'*.

Yet if you hope, Hope does not disappoint you!

> This is why it says: "When he ascended on high, he led captives in his train and gave gifts to men." (What does "he ascended" mean except that he also descended to the lower, earthly regions? He who descended is the one who ascended higher than all the heavens, in order to fill the whole universe.) It was he who gave some to be apostles, some to be prophets, some to be evangelists, and some to be pastors and teachers, to prepare God's people for works of service, so that the body of Christ may be built up until we all reach unity in the faith and in the knowledge of the Son of God and become mature, attaining to the whole measure of the fullness of Christ,"
>
> (Ephesians 4:8, NIV)

Treasure in the darkness

In the void, is a priceless promise for all of those who go down to the end of themselves and find a richer, precious experience of peace in God. Now there is a rest in Him that is nothing to do with the circumstances. You can submit to the fact of incapability and descend into your own inadequacy to discover that the real way of escape is often farther below, more profound and more inaccessible than anything one could ever lose or fear.

Jesus descended so that we could ascend and *there is no place lower than where he has already been.* If there were, everybody there would be beyond his reach.

There is no character too depraved, no sinner too sinful, no action too powerful to cut anyone from God if the person can accept they want Him there. And the great news for visionaries held in some grip of doubt and fear is this: there is no call too impossible that God will not equip you for; that He would ask of you without providing a way of escape for it.

> *"No temptation has overtaken you that is not common to man. God is faithful, and he will not let you be tempted beyond your ability, but with the temptation, he will also provide the way of escape, that you may be able to endure it"*
>
> (1 Corinthians 10:13, ESV)

So, it is not the circumstances that you should rail against or elevate, it is your response to them that defines you and your way of escape. You are not meant to have to learn the hard way by shame or disgrace or losses that might have been avoided by making wise choices in life. I know God does not mean you to learn that way. He is a good Father and would want you to learn quickly and easily and access His blessings as soon as possible.

Brokenness is to cry to God *"Show me your ways. I need you, I need you, I need you so much…God, I need you so much!"*

This was the cry of my heart for at least a year and a half. I would find every day that I could not come into the presence of God without dissolving into tears. I could only cry out for help and mercy in my desperate need and exhausted resource of human strength and inspiration. Even with every attempt to release energy and reduce my commitments, the burden seemed to grow and crush me more heavily than ever. I felt unable to halt a slow but inexorable slide into depression and anxiety. All my relationships were jaded and strained, and I was falling into the refuge of self-absorption and self-analysis to the point of confusion and despair. I feared I would become a shadow of myself, a wretched and failed example, even insane.

As the days grew darker and my fight intensified, a rarely induced laugh would cause me a bursting, searing pain and pressure in the nape of my neck and skull. Though I carefully presented myself, I felt disengaged from others' needs, their joys. Even the sunshine, small moments of pleasure or blessing merely activated regret. It was a void, and like Joe, I shouted frantically for 'Simon' to no avail.

'Simon' had long gone; thinking me shattered and dead.

But not God

I kept reaching for a miracle until one spring day in 2007 I meditated upon this Scripture.

> But as for me, I will look expectantly for the Lord and with confidence in Him I will keep watch; I will wait with confident expectation for the God of my salvation. My God will hear me.

> (Micah 7:7)

Painstakingly, I started to move into a new and a special grace upon my life.

I determined to have a two-week total abstinence from negative words and thoughts, I spoke the word and promises, used the weapons of warfare and the power of praise. All of which, God had been drawing my attention to. This was against the backdrop of being transformed from my church-centred (or even church-driven) lifestyle to a God seeking and God-centred heart. Add to this a stirring commitment to serve and to love those closest to me despite my dullness of heart.

God's work in me was all wrapped up in those inner changes starting to take place in me and in my relationships. To this day I rejoice in His patience and grace over me even as He was about to allow me to be marked by the trial of a catastrophic loss.

It would bring liberty to my continuing journey.

The flood

Now I know just how much God was going to achieve through this next loss I cannot describe it any other way than merely the end of an era. The morning I saw for myself the devastation twenty-four hours of solid rain had brought to Marsh Gate, Doncaster, I knew an escape route I had never expected or wanted had suddenly opened.

Our church building sat under two feet of river water. That meant months of clearance, disposal, reclamation…or resignation. The police prohibited any access, and all we could do was retreat, stare into our coffee cup confusedly and ponder 'Why?' For a couple of emergency weeks, we felt our hearts stirred by compassion toward others whose lives and homes had been torn apart. Indeed, we re-located our core people and salvaged our focus onto the community most hard-hit by this flood. We engaged in some of the most exciting and radical outreach I had ever done.

I kept asking God "what now?" more quietly now, more humbly, less self-centredly. We were on the ledge that broke our calamitous fall. Broken, re-orientating and rejoicing, we were in a void, but we were still. However, the longer-term outlook was threatening. Let me say that a realisation came that there was no further grace to fight. I finally allowed the inevitable rolling off from my ledge of tiring self-effort and back up plans.

I resigned.

God allowed me to experience the disintegration of ministry, marriage, emotions and occupation (the story is told more fully elsewhere)[5]. That day I let go and rolled into the abyss. Like the scene from The Last of the Mohicans where Alice wordlessly steps off the mountain path as the savage Magua leans forward to claim her as his own[6]. I ascribed to God His position as God and Lord. I stepped back from the deceptive allure of ministry's insatiable demand upon me.

> "So they will fear the name of the Lord from the west
> And His glory from the rising of the sun.
> For He will come in like a narrow, rushing stream
> Which the breath of the Lord drives overwhelming
> the enemy. "A Redeemer (Messiah) will come to Zion,
> And to those in Jacob (Israel) who turn from
> transgression (sin)," declares the Lord.
> "As for Me, this is My covenant with them," says the
> Lord: "My Spirit which is upon you writing the law of
> God on the heart, and My words which I have put in
> your mouth shall not depart from your mouth, nor
> from the mouths of your true, spiritual children, nor
> from the mouth of your children's children," says the
> Lord, "from now and forever."
> "Arise from spiritual depression to a new life, shine
> be radiant with the glory and brilliance of the Lord;
> for your light has come,
> And the glory and brilliance of the Lord has risen
> upon you"

(Isaiah 59:19- 60:1)

I stand amazed at the way God would take the foolish things of this world and shame the wise. I celebrate what God has done, overcoming family manipulation, marital discord, estrangement and divorce. God saw in me a woman of spiritual stature, refusal to be defined or contained by those who squashed and resisted or tried to control her. My weaknesses became my greatest strength because they refused me the comfort of any provider other than God Himself who now directly and richly supplies all my needs.

> *"Show me your ways, O LORD, teach me your paths; guide me in your truth and teach me, for you are God my Saviour, and my hope is in you all day long"*
>
> (Psalm 25:4, NIV)

As *your* alabaster box is broken, then everything you are, everything you would be and every means to get there is given into the hands of Him alone who can do this. Then a precious flow leaks out and all you must do is allow it to be lavishly released as an attractive anointing.

The lock gates open

First the underwater sluice gates are opened. The water levels lower in the lock even before the gates are prised apart. Something has given deep inside. A secret submission has taken place, and the resistance is drained.

The edges of the lock-gates creep apart and the residual column in the water table arcs into the lower lock, measured and controlled by the speed of the gate and the watchful eye of the lock keeper. The cascade of tea-like fluid escapes as a metaphorical cascade of generosity, humility, and love instead of sparingly measured with restraint, miserliness and begrudging.

Brokenness is allowing the character of Christ to flow through and conquer the temptation to make your own assessment of the value of what you are doing. This is on the way to getting there and even after arriving. And brokenness is making an *'as if'* faith assessment of what you have and who you are - with certainty, long before the appearance of physical or evidence that most testimonials rely on.

I even write about it now, and you see it, as I do.

As if it had already happened!

CHAPTER 8
THE WEAKEST LINK

Casting off from our moorings in the now thickly wooded belt of trees, we start again the following afternoon, having had to wait hours for a neighbourly boat tripper to sell us some fuel. About halfway between the three and five rise staircases, I navigate the waterway, screened by mature oaks and beech trees; dappled light filtering onto the khaki waters. Entering an arched green tunnel flanked by the broad trunks of matured deciduous woodland, light plays on the narrowboat roof. We round the bend to see the imposing height of the Bingley Five rise staircase.

Contrasting with the muted landscape, stark black and white railings and cross beams are hatched in a geometric mesh of rectangles, against a cobalt block of sky, exaggerated by its deep reflection in the calm basin. I am buoyed by the victory of the Bingley 3-rise, a sense of confidence and trust in the lock-keeper's watchful guidance and the principles of engineering. This means, despite my tiredness this time I feel am far better prepared to progress with confidence.

The Leaking Lock

I had a somewhat absent-minded friend, a businesswoman and a member of the church, two years into a new relationship with God. She'd had a strained relationship with her natural father as a child. His weekending parental responsibilities as a divorcee were alarmingly casual. For my friend to have survived without incident was remarkable. Yet, I observed a resultant flatness and expressive reserve in her. She was growing in this journey of comprehending God's love for herself, against the backdrop of painfully learned self-sufficiency.

During one overcast, wet June day set aside for study, writing inspiration was lacking. I could not seem to jump-start or resume the flow that had petered out a couple of months earlier. I visited her home three streets away from mine. Returning her mislaid mobile phone was an excellent opportunity to breathe fresh air and gave God a chance to surprise me.

This morning, right on cue she played into the hands of God. He was able to unlock something as she related an insight that dawned upon my outlook. We chatted about the challenge of taking authority over the tyranny of small things. God was provoking me about such things as the washing, the piles of ironing, and failing to get to bed on time. Or the natural tendency to criticise or failure to greet one's nearest and dearest with as much honour as an occasional guest.

She told me that in the 1980's as a member of the CB radio community, her pseudonym was 'Cosmic Lady' as she was into astrology at the time. She related that what we believe about ourselves is what we project in our self-presentation and our home-life. What people see of us is a valid and unique interpretation and not necessarily what we think we are projecting (I squirmed).

She was learning to take pride in her appearance not because this is the goal, but it is one means to the end of winning people (especially her husband) and being Christ-like to those we meet. She described a powerful analogy drawn from astronomy. Of all the stellar constellations, she always looked for the familiar Plough amongst the night sky. I agreed. It is the only one I can easily identify. But she asked me, what if I stood at a different point in space and then looked for the Plough?

It would not look the same.

Those stars can only be drawn together as a plough from an earthborn perspective. Similarly, God views our lives from a different perspective and sees us as a constellation of a very different nature. God looks from a heavenly place, and it is in His eyes, we are what we really are.

I mused on this as I returned to my laptop that day.
What if I looked at others as God sees them, at myself as God sees me? That's what He'd been trying to show me all along. That's where my passion for the lost was invigorated, and that's where my energy for the ministry was sustained.

That is where any conviction about *all things being possible* is to be sourced.

Perspective is the weakest link

Your limited perspective is the weakest link in the journey of God's purposes being fulfilled in your life and constellation of relationships. Your perspective is the breakdown or the disconnection between God's actual provision for you and your experience of His favour. In my life there was a considerable disconnection between His *"so loving the world that he gave His only Son"* and my feeling loved.

Jesus' patient ministry to his own disciples constantly linked them to a distant world apart, a different perspective and a Kingdom mentality. Three years in, they still struggled to comprehend it. Similarly, God's gift of connection to Himself through His own Son Jesus is ever threatened and vulnerable to your own self-effort, misunderstanding, ignorance, analysis, and rejection.

> *"Who then can be saved?"*
> *Jesus looked at them and said, "With man this is impossible, but with God all things are possible." Peter answered him, "We have left everything to follow you! What then will there be for us?" Jesus said to them, "I tell you the truth, at the renewal of all things, when the Son of Man sits on his glorious throne, you who have followed me will also sit on twelve thrones, judging the twelve tribes of Israel."*

> (Matthew 19:25-28, NIV)

For most of the human population, there is a weak link between the offer of inclusive and perfect salvation and the acceptance and uptake of this marvellous life. I saw that this weak link of my feeble perspective of my Life and me and of Him (and yes in that order) had been sabotaging His wonderful purposes all my life. Regarding my own mental software programming, there was a *'fatal error in my application'*.

But now He was showing me that I could stand in a new place, and I did not have to do anything more except revisit my life and operate afresh, from a new vantage point. I could live my life now, *as if* He can do the impossible because from His place it is all so possible. Only from God's place is the detail significant. How a friend, neighbour or even a spouse views you is never as important as how you are viewed by God.

Although I appeared cool calm, collected and prosperous to the majority who were not looking too closely, my veneer was wearing thin. The frustrations were pressing in and the emotions harder and harder to manage. God showed me that my immense passion for Him and His purposes, the grand scale of what I yearned for within my lifetime and scope of influence for good would fall far short if I did not attend to the small stuff. Big dreaming, 'head-in-the-clouds' Gill would have to knuckle down to the minutiae of family life for God to have His way in me.

I had been impossibly wedged in, bottlenecked somewhere between my call and destiny by my narrow view of what concerned God!

Finding a way of escape was in seeing the predicament from God's viewpoint.

I had been caught for months and years in a weak link somewhere between my call and my destiny.

> "His feet they hurt with fetters; he was laid in chains of iron and his soul entered into the iron."

> (Psalm 105:18)

My physical circumstances had been fettered but worse, my perspective was bound. My soul, (mind, will, and emotions) my soul, came into the bondage of limitation. Fear and control bound me in a cage of iron.

However, that happens to your soul, the truth is: grace will lay it open again.

You only need to trust in a much higher level of wisdom than your own earthbound, reactive version.

Lock-keeper leans over the first footbridge, ascertaining that we are ready for the ascent. He will instruct and guide my partner on the opposite bank, and I must steer the tiller as he instructs me in locking up. The lock ahead is empty, so he opens the first gates, and I drive straight in. He closes the bottom gates and paddles, advising me to stay at the lowest end of the lock. Opening the paddles ahead, he watches the rising levels as I gently rock. He has positioned me so that the narrowboat is prevented from buffeting and drifting at a diagonal within the pound as the waters rise. He understands how to pin the vessel parallel to the wall and harness rather than resist the currents entering the pound as the paddles and gates are then opened. I recognise that our safe and easeful passage is determined by his expertise and not our own. Experience may bring anticipation, but this is a working relationship that safeguards even the most inexperienced or incapable narrow boat pilot.

So here was a lifesaving insight. The healing of my emotional torment, long exhausted passion and forensically examined motives was merely this.

To agree with everything, He says I am and will become. Yes, to trust Him and His perspective. To receive His grace, His power made perfect in my weakness!

> *"So that [the genuineness] of your faith may be tested, [your faith] which is infinitely more precious than the perishable gold which is tested and purified by fire. [This proving of your faith is intended] to redound to [your] praise and glory and honour when Jesus Christ (the Messiah, the Anointed One) is revealed."*
>
> (1 Peter 1:7)

Progressive potential rather than obstructive delay

I came to understand this as a breakthrough insight.
Delay caused by an obstructive lock is the potential for
higher progress. Seeing the lock as a means to elevate
you to a higher plane rather than opposing you, is a
crucial step in embracing rather than recoiling from life's
challenges. What clearer picture could you have than this
simple engineering solution? Man-made waterways climb
and descend nature's topographical features. Yet for all its
ingenuity, canal engineering remains dependent upon its
continuous supply of water.

Access to summit reservoirs

This necessity remained one of the engineering challenges
of the eighteenth and nineteenth centuries in ensuring a
navigable waterway for the uninterrupted flow of traffic
and conveyance of coal, lime, wool, cotton and even
manure. Throughout its active evolution, demands upon
the Leeds-Liverpool canal continued to press its engineers in
sourcing or improving access to the summit reservoirs from
which over a hundred and eighty-eight million gallons of
water flowed. Enough to fill two and a half thousand locks!

Consequently, water conservation was the prime
consideration for its designers, users, and shareholders.
The canals' navigability and profitability depended upon
continuous supply and judicious use.

Today, waterway etiquette is lasting evidence of this
important consideration. Pilots consider how to leverage one
another's impact upon the opening and closing of lock
gates at the same time. Wherever a vessel passes another
in the opposite direction, it is vital to determine whether
an approaching boat can use the water one may be about
to drain.

Conversely, God's grace is also available to us in many situations because of other's consideration or just because there is an endless and replenishing supply from the summit of His throne. When valued and cherished, responsibly channelled and stewarded, God's grace offers life, buoyancy, and momentum to a route previously impassable or frustrating. Without His infilling and enabling and, to some degree, the timing and generosity of others' inclusion, the fluid of His life in us and our life in Him—our purposes—are beached.

The weakest link in a canal is any pound that has drained too much. It becomes unnavigable and neglected, even falling into disrepair.

Are you are caught in the silt of the canal bed, scraping along with significant risk and consequent damage to the underbelly of your hull? Barely able to endeavour anything meaningful again you flail around in the mud of your own ability until grace, His wonderful buffer, His generous equipping gift swirls around and lifts your stricken vessel once again.

"you receive the result (outcome, consummation) of your faith, the salvation of your souls".

(1 Peter 1:9 AMPC)

How is faith consummated?

The canal link is the connection of the distance between Leeds and Liverpool. Right between the start and finish and all along the watercourse is the union of your call and destiny. It represents the consummation of faith. It is the union of Christ and the church which is me and you. His water of life flows and courses through the path of God's destiny as you point the prow forward again.

That course is the salvation of the soul.

The mind becomes the mind of Christ, the emotions are subject to Him, and one's decisions are made according to His will, His revealed will which is called the Word.

> *"Christ loved the church and gave himself up for her to make her holy, cleansing her by the washing with water through the word, and to present her to himself as a radiant church, without stain or wrinkle or any other blemish, but holy and blameless."*
>
> (Ephesians 5:25-27, NIV)

This is pictured in the resting of your boat upon the waterway. In this place of rest, you are given to the washing of the water of the Word. It solves the weakness you face in traversing such a distance. Your dependence upon the water's transmitting power remains throughout the journey's length. The engagement of faith to trust the carrying force must be applied from start to finish. Throughout a horizontal journey in time the water-filled channel of your weakness in His strength remains a continuous connection by the consummation of our faith.

It is the ultimate, intimate communion.

It is the union of your call and destiny.

SITTING - BRIDGE

YOU ACQUIESCE "EVEN IF!"
YOU REST, AS IF ALL IS ACCOMPLISHED

"Esau said, "Let us be on our way; I'll accompany you."

But Jacob said to him, "My lord knows that the children are tender and that I must care for the ewes and cows that are nursing their young. If they are driven hard just one day, all the animals will die.

So let my lord go on ahead of his servant, while I move along at the pace of the droves before me and that of the children, until I come to my lord in Seir."

Esau said, "Then let me leave some of my men with you." "But why do that?" Jacob asked. "Just let me find favour in the eyes of my lord."

So that day Esau started on his way back to Seir.

Jacob, however, went to Succoth, where he built a place for himself and made shelters for his livestock. That is why the place is called Succoth.

After Jacob came from Paddan Aram, he arrived safely at the city of Shechem in Canaan and camped within sight of the city.

For a hundred pieces of silver, he bought from the sons of Hamor, the father of Shechem, the plot of ground where he pitched his tent.

There he set up an altar and called it El Elohe Israel."

(Genesis 33:12–20, NIV)

Take me home - to the place I belong.

We have had quite enough drama for one day. Trea and I should have been home for a family dinner a couple of hours ago.

"Are you mad with me?" Trea tests, somewhat uneasily.

Long past our expected arrival time, I recognise that we still need to take a moment to gather our thoughts, look into each other's eyes and make sure we have absorbed the lesson we have just been a party to.

Trea's ability to accept and believe there is nothing further to resolve, is still tender and vulnerable to misunderstanding. I want her to be certain that we are straight with each other. All is forgiven, yet she must know she cannot risk her safety or my sanity again in this way.

We sit in the back seat of the car for a few minutes, rocking in each other's arms until, finally, a murmur becomes a giggle that explodes into a gale of laughter.

We are OK. She knows that however I explain this to her parents, she will be exonerated. Relief beams all over her yellow street-lamp lit face, and she eagerly nods at my suggestion of a pit-stop bag of hot chips to keep us going.

Before I have even left the neighbourhood and set the car west, she is lolling sleepily against me and I reduce the selected speed to a more comfortable level. I am assured of a peaceful journey and express thankfulness within my heart for Trea's safety.

Relishing the independence, my autonomous vehicle has afforded me this last decade I also sit back appreciatively for the few miles we have to cover. Ironically, the only way

I can enjoy the independence of night driving at my age is because I have put my faith and total trust in this technology.

A worthwhile risk indeed.

CHAPTER 9
ACCEPTANCE: THE ADOPTED ORPHAN

As the towering lock gates close in on me and the windlass ratchet grates above, my mate disappears, and I cannot hear instructions from the kerb. I panic, and I rail against the intimidating enclosure and crane my neck to see where I might find a ladder or foothold. I know I must escape; the prospect of five more locks is overwhelming.

Anguish grips me over my urge to abandon the boat and abort the mission. There is a disruption to the route and other travellers, the failure of this trip and financial waste of investment into it. I think the lock keeper must meet this kind of trepidation all the time but mine is a concealed, profoundly disrupted confidence. I know he is here to help me, and I am the reason he is at this spot. Yet he watches me scale the ladder and seems to be at ease about me abandoning the narrowboat behind.

I run to the wooded fringes of the towpath. Tripping over brambles, catching nettles and nearly rupturing my ankle in a rabbit hole, I crash upon a strewn bough in a mossy coppice, coming to an ungainly and abrupt halt amongst the tender bluebells. After a series of rustling disturbances settles into a thick silence, I turn to catch sight and attend to a curtain of sparkling dust specks in a diagonal beam of brilliant light breaking through the canopy above. Capturing my attention, I hold my gaze for a few timeless moments, losing touch with the pressing realities of a few moments before. I notice alarmed calls and demands from my fellow passenger back on the waterway. I remember that look of total understanding that the Lock-keeper threw me, and I stay rooted to the broad, solid bed of earth supporting my body, remaining motionless, blocking out the obligatory urges to reply. As my eyelids partially close, a melee of dancing blue globes swells and shrinks, enhancing the sense of unreality, contrasting with the darkness of the lock well and confusion of my urgent flight. Absconding like this was unrehearsed, uncharacteristic and unbelievable to everyone that knew me, or thought they did! But the Lock-keeper, or God the Father, had seen it all before and he knew it was the start of something new.

He let me walk away because he knew I was walking straight into His arms.

Lock of Acceptance

Life became an escalating succession of losses.

It had been such an energetic start, but already we were faltering. I had prayed for faith and trust but what was the answer to my prayers? In facing my stark incapacity and mountain of gruelling church leadership obstacles, I was to be taken to the extreme of losing all but hope in God.

In the spring of 2008, I was faced with the fact that my life was not in what I did or what people thought of me, or even how much I was loved and appreciated by others. One sultry evening at the end of a rare and extravagant trip with my children to Alton Towers, the rock band *Delerious?*[1] played.

Tears streamed down my face as they ushered in the presence of angels like a cluster of fireflies. Reflecting on the audience on the big screen, a bobbing sea of mobile phone lights played across the open-air crowd. Then, as if prophetically singing over the irresolvable discord between my husband and me and the imminent breakdown of all we had worked for, *Delerious?* belted out,

> *"One thing I have pondered*
> *How the mighty fall,*
> *I've sung the songs of heaven*
> *Just to lose it all*
> *See me falling down*
> *See me falling down*
> *Another day in paradise*
> *Another day to die*
> *The writing's on the wall again*
> *The future's asking why*
> *Why we turned away*
> *Why we turn away*
> *Is there, is there a place*
> *In your arms of love?*
> *Strong enough*
> *Will you carry us, carry us?*
> *...Stare the monster down!*
> *Stare the monster down!*

It was a picture of great emotional devastation and brokenness.

I had already lost my courage and joy.

I had lost my fight for the dream to help steer a church toward great influence for the kingdom. I had lost trust by, and in, my husband and I had lost my support network, primarily as I lost my vital lifelong friend and those associated with her. I felt I had lost my reputation and purpose, my vision and perspective.

Almost overnight all developmental work, meaningful activity, appointments, plans, meetings, preparation, visits and calls, emails, texts, strategic thought, influence, responsibility and accountability to others disappeared. I was left with a clean-up of paperwork and loose ends that reflected the previous years' summer flooding.

And God still loved me.

This I knew, and in the blur of it all, I knew that it would all come right somehow. Even so, I didn't even want to live any longer. Not with the separation, shame, and stain of failure and presumable indictment.

Who would phone me now, who would offer comfort?

Who was even allowed to reach out their hand due to unreasonable restrictions erected around my life?
What sense of accomplishment could there be?
What joy of imparted hope or insight could I now find?
Through teaching or explaining or by sensing any lift of the Holy Spirit?

I wandered around my vacant life trying to locate a reference for what was happening.

Disintegrating

I knew activity didn't create one's sense of self or value. I valued work for what it would achieve rather than as an end. However, it had still shaped my spirituality in an unhealthy way and left a daily residue in my spirit of unworthiness and inability as I fell for the lie that one day I would finish what had to be done.

Even while I resented the sheer effort everything seemed to cost me. I had no other strategy. Such an approach had to peter out somewhere, and this was it. This was the end of independence, self-effort, slavish expression of allegiance rather than love and a desperate need to achieve, to arrive and to do everything I believed I should.

This was the day I felt, rather than merely knew, the primary value of my role as a daughter to Him. Friend, wife, mother, pastor, sister, these were all roles I held. Some enduring and some, time-limited - and all ultimately temporal.

But to be a daughter, a child of God is a relationship that stands for all eternity. I couldn't do anything for Him anymore. Whatever had made me think I could? It was only ever about what He could do for me. I had served and sacrificed and donated and pursued and persevered, but suddenly I had stopped, and He was saying *"Receive!*

Receive and be changed in receiving not achieving. Your only success is in knowing Me, and all your motivations are subtly changed and endued with power and strength".

> *"Of the increase of his government and peace there will be no end."*

> (Isaiah 9:7, NIV)

"Yes, as Father, your care will bring me to that place of total rest I have yearned for. Father not Master or even Lord, but Father" I replied.

You are my Rock, my comfort, my source, and strength. Oh, to live in this place always sure of your acceptance and unconditional love. This was my more profound understanding. He wants us to abide, but when we search too hard, we miss the way there.

Lovers of God

Jesus exhorted His disciples to love one another as His primary example to the world so they would see we are lovers of God. Knowing that they would face testing and confusion, He confronted them with a challenge. He asked if they would lay down their lives for Him. They were sorely tested before they understood the value of loving Him freely[2].

John, Chapter 14 is a heart appeal from the Son of God to understand the nature of the Father's gracious provision to help us. The chapter is an endorsement of all His assistance provided for them and for us in advance. It spurs, encourages and guides us.

It begins and ends with exhortations to be at peace as Jesus shows the power of His life in the Father.

> *"Do not let your hearts be troubled. Trust in God; trust also in me...."*.

> (John 14:1, NIV)

> *"Peace I leave with you; my peace I give you. I do not give to you as the world gives. Do not let your hearts be troubled and do not be afraid."*

> (John 14:27, NIV)

He paints a picture of the end of life so that we can see what is to come as if it already is.

> *"In my Father's house are many rooms; if it were not so, I would have told you. I am going there to prepare*

a place for you. And if I go and prepare a place for you, I will come back and take you to be with me that you also may be where I am."

(John 14:2-3 NIV)

In the following two verses Jesus says that if we know Him, we will get to the right destination. There isn't anything else we need to know.

Here is a picture of the waterway

Canals were first dug out by hand by the navvies under gruelling conditions in a different industrial era. They were the equivalent of the forefathers of the faith who paid such a high price for our freedom. It was filthy, back-breaking work.

Once dug, they lined the channels with waterproof clay. They called this laborious and messy process of pounding and sealing water and clay "puddling". The waterway of salvation was cut by God then made watertight by the perfect life, love, and sacrifice of Jesus who is the Way the Truth and the Life[3].

Wherever the Father goes - wherever the course of the canal cuts - around or through the hills and vales, Jesus goes too. He is in the Father. And we know the Father through Jesus. We follow the Father by following Jesus, the sure and certain and infallible Way. When we follow Jesus, we are following and knowing the Father. Even if we feel we have never seen him, we are in Him.

How we need to know this Fatherhood in our lives. Just as Philip asked to see him, not realising he had already been looking at Him, we realise there has been an accessible and continuous intimacy available to us all along.

We might start believing in the works of Jesus, but these were only ever meant to be a starting point progressing us along to actual belief in the Father - in Himself. Not just His works, or the works He wants to perform in and through us.

> *"Believe Me that I am in the Father and the Father in Me; or else believe Me for the very [works] themselves. [If you cannot trust Me, at least let these works that I do in My Father's name convince you.]"*

(John 14:11)

And then follows a wonderful promise.

Understand that the nature of this Father-Son relationship is based upon approval, delight, and desire to bless and pour out lavish affection. As we approach this same mutual Father in Jesus, we can ask anything we desire. We can come to Him with the same expectation and total confidence in acceptance as if we are Jesus.

> *"as presenting all that I AM!"*

(John 14:13)

Only then the obstacle, the lock in the waterway will open, and we realise that He could not open it until we had risen to the equivalent height of that place we aimed for. He has taken all the drama out of the transition. Instead of lock gates belching out gallons of water upon the vulnerable vessel below, the water tables are equalised, and she simply sails through. Spectators would find the careless approach far more exciting, but thankfully, it is not the way God leads his children.

He offers the help of the Holy Spirit, the Comforter, the one who remains with you forever, opening the way, handling the timing and cues, assisting and enabling you in your journey. His job may look mundane and even easy. Casual observers would not even recognise his skill.

> "But you know and recognise Him, for He lives with you [constantly] and will be in you"

> (John 14:17)

> "He will teach you all things. And He will cause you to recall (will remind you of, bring to remembrance) everything I have told you"

> (John14:26)

Yes, He, the Holy Spirit will help you to attain to new heights, new levels in Christ.

Knowing He will do this brings peace – an inheritance - a gift from your brother Jesus. Notice that He brings to remembrance what Jesus has already told you. So, if you recall what Jesus has told you then now you can live the reality. What He had once said, you are now living. The Holy Spirit is integral to your ability to grasp the means to live *now* with faith and confidence.

As if the Truth *will* come to pass!

> "And I have told you this before it occurs, so that when it does take place you may believe and have faith in and rely on Me"

> (John 14: 29)

Then comes the crux of it all.
There is the intimate discovery that this is all because you now irrevocably belong to Him.

"I will not leave you as orphans [comfortless, desolate, bereaved, forlorn, helpless] I will come [back] to you"

(John 14:18)

This is the moment when you know you have all the backing of heaven, all the acceptance you will ever need. You have all the encouragement of a Father with you overlooking your fault and failure just because you are His. You are the epicentre of all His attention.

The canal is filled with water, the life of the living Word fills and carries the traveller along the course marked out for him. The narrowboat is floated by its pressure and force and the integrity of the lining.

"I am in My Father, and you [are] in Me and I [am] in you"

(John 14:20)

You are the vessel

I had thought that the vessel was the church I helped to lead. I had believed that the ministry and its safe passage was my primary concern as navigator of the boat that sailed the Leeds - Liverpool canal. For all her importance, it was a distorted perception of my call. Even when I laid her down, never for a moment was I running from God. I continued to love Him with all my heart and despite my deepest despair and shame. I may have had to abandon this boat but God, my own Father, was about to reveal something incredible.

I can love the cause without needing to be the cause

Strains of frustrated exclamations and resigned catcalls drift through the trees to where I lie, stock still, wild grasses tickling my nostrils. When they are almost

despairing of my return, I emerge from the thickets, descend to the vessel and take the tiller once again.

I realise the vessel is a picture of me, *not* the church I am leading. I accept that the confidence of the Lock-keeper is enough for my safe passage. I root myself inside the cabin. Lock-keeper will take me through.

I am not interrupting other concerns of His and yet, I am the focus of all His expertise this lazy afternoon. Now I know He will ensure that I safely and triumphantly rise to new heights beyond these sequential tests.

So, having found the strength to embrace intimacy with Him for the journey, there was no doubt I should take back my God-given opportunity to sail on. The service of a cause is a beautiful thing, but first He is the one in whom we live and breathe. Then we find direction again into a specific outworking of love in Him.

> *"Because you are sons, God sent the Spirit of his Son into our hearts, the Spirit who calls out, "Abba, Father". So you are no longer a slave, but a son; and since you are a son, God has made you also an heir"*

> (Galatians 4:6-7, NIV)

Now I am a daughter, not a servant or even a favoured friend.

His very own daughter.

This is the one enduring role in life which connects me and you to all other eternal relationships.

CHAPTER 10
HOPE - AGAINST ALL HOPE!

The heavy gates close in again. Token spillage from the pound above spurts over the stern. Dripping willow-herb and mosses line the walls. I rock as the waters surge up from beneath. Rising to eye level with groups of Sunday strollers, I sense elation that this is happening so straightforwardly. The Lock keeper monitors the rising levels and the cue for the facing gate to be opened, allowing us forward to the next pound, first checking the lower gate is sealed.

My partner works under the guidance of the ruddy-faced bobble-hatted Lock keeper who is short on words other than curt timely warnings, alerting ignorant observers from dangers of being caught between the beam and the kerb, or from standing too close to the edge. Lock keeper's eyes dart backward, across then ahead. He strides across the footbridge and back down the steep stone steps, returning to advise again.

He understands so much more than is clear of the circumstances, suggesting an ease and grace which belies my previous lock passage experiences. He suggests we open the gate only halfway which is more than enough width to pass and reduces the effort of re-securing the lock. It strikes me that this studious and weather-beaten man is both aware of the detailed consecutive risks and has an understated grasp of the effective harnessing of the water table along with the timing of vessels' etiquette and passage priority.

The Vacuum Lock

Nature hates a vacuum.

God cannot resist a spirit that is hungry and thirsty after Him. Your hopeful hunger creates a vacuum that sucks Him into it, into a spiritual atmosphere of communion you naturally need. But it hurts to live with this kind of holy discontent, and you prefer to fill it with other things that dull the pain. There is also a risk that the discontent or firestorm of frustration[1] (as Bill Hybels once called it,) may begin eating away at your hope.

The enemy of faith and hope

Maybe you question *'Could my dream really happen?'* This is what foxes you. Or you ask, *'Have I been playing a waiting game for so many years, even decades?'*. That was my mistake. I tried to make it happen because my miracle was taking so long.

Proverbs 1:31 says *"they will eat the fruit of their ways and be filled with the fruit of their schemes."*

Even though intended for God, the fruit of my schemes was total exhaustion and utter frustration. These two are the enemy of faith and hope.

A need, however small or unspoken, is a reminder of His care and concern and our utter reliance upon Him for life and health and strength and even the ability to hope.

So, my recognition of the need for a complete and absolute dependence was a breakthrough. Once, I would have thought to myself, 'How ridiculous to pray to God about a shopping trip or a parking space'. I would only ask Him about *real* needs.

This was where God took me and my deep, unfulfilled needs over the course of the next two years. I came to the point that I would melt with gratitude upon waking to clear blue skies and the song of a blackbird. This was even while I was scraping an existence on a paltry family income supplemented by government tax reliefs. Facing deadline after deadline when the money would expire, or the cost of living would exceed my diminishing reserve, I became attuned to the value of each unique day, much as a cancer patient uncertain of their prognosis appreciates each moment and interaction with a new intensity.

I had spent years of pushing in my own strength.

Exhausted in my own natural ability, launching into a self-fuelled type of faith was doomed because it had no solid anchor in time of trouble. Faith must be anchored in a fixed and immovable base. I came to understand how vital God's supply of strength was to my life.

Hebrews 11:3 explains that what we see was made from invisible, hoped for things, not things that are visible. If you *have* faith, this proves the existence of the thing you cannot see. You only hope for what you *do not* have. Hope, therefore, precedes faith.

Without hope, there is no need for faith.
Without hope, faith cannot be activated.

Without a need, there is no need for hope.
So, without a need, hope will not be activated.

When you are capable, effective and self-sufficient, you are outside of the domain of hope and faith. You do not even consider the relevance of God. So, for some, God allows a depth of need to open, so acute that it can only be termed a kind of suffering. Suffering is a common theme or optimum condition that can accelerate the growth of faith in a Christian.

If there's one thing I have learned about this faith journey, it is that I have often forgotten more than I know about what God is doing. In other words, He has often already said enough for me to step forward with confidence. And even when I step forward on the strength of it, I see with hindsight many other words He has spoken already have re-appeared to instill a fresh new life. The power and directive strength of those words were always there, but sometimes only hindsight reminded me of that.

Now with the benefit of hindsight, I want to introduce some of those words.

God's own whispers were graciously sent to secure in me a confidence that almost slipped through my fingers. Recurring forgetfulness about these words almost led me to self-inflicted despair and defeat. That would have been my own choice through negligence and rebellion by underestimating the power of the words that took me so long to wield as spoken swords of faith.

Abraham was commended by God. He was a man that God deemed righteous because of his faith and yet he too displayed some of these forgetful traits.

> *"Now faith is being sure of what we hope for and certain of what we do not see"*

> (Hebrews 11:1, NIV)

Surely that statement gives you hope?

What you now see was once made of invisible, hoped for things. I wanted to be counted as a woman of faith. So, if I had faith, its existence proved there must be an object of it (which also exists).

> *"By faith we understand that the universe was formed at God's command, so that what is seen was not made out of what was visible"*

(Hebrews 11:3, NIV)

Similarly, what you cannot see, yet hope for will yet become visible. Hebrews 11:6 emphasises that faith is a thing that God rewards. These rewards are the inheritance of the promise which is believed in. What a chapter Hebrews 11 is!

Divine approval

The overwhelming message is not merely that you will see the fulfilment of your faith, but that faith ensures something even more precious. Faith assures divine approval. For a person like me who was years down the track of being weaned off the need for human approval, the possibility of divine approval sounded like a breath of fresh air.

John 11:40 says that I will see his glory if I believe. If I need help with my faith, I need to know what weakens and strengthens it. I must go back a few pages before the famous passage known as the Hebrews Hall of Fame to find out where these heroes of faith were schooled and entrusted with their monster-sized faith. One thing I know for sure that does not precede or establish faith is the activity of my own strength or the *works of the flesh* as the traditional Bibles put it.

"For God is not unrighteous to forget or overlook your labour and the love which you have shown for His name's sake in ministering to the needs of the saints (His own consecrated people), as you still do. But we do [strongly and earnestly] desire for each of you to show the same diligence and sincerity [all the way through] in realising and enjoying the full assurance and development of [your] hope until the end"

(Hebrews 6:10-11)

If I had invested as much sincerity and diligence into the assurance and development of hope as I did toward my ministry, I would have been secure.

If I had nurtured my own life, as much as I nurtured the vision, the mission, the programmes, and activities, then I would have been strong. What a hard-won lesson this was for me.

I became so weary.

The writer of Hebrews encourages you too, to imitate those who lean their whole personality on God in Christ, in absolute trust and confidence and in His power, wisdom, and goodness by waiting and enduring with patience.

Why? These are the Christ followers who inherited their dreams and promises.

If you imitate them- you too will inherit!

Just how did they develop hope?

Take Abraham. Like him, they experienced a delay of endurance and development of patience which is a characteristic of any great go-getter in God. There is no quick way of learning this. God is so determined that we do not cheat. Any attribute worth having will be expensive. But waiting, of itself, is not the secret.

No, it is who we are waiting for.
That is the nourishment of hope and, consequently, faith.

Hebrews 6:18 states that God cannot change what He has promised to those He has promised it. So, what has He promised? (We are picking up the scent of a certain hope here). His promise is the *"un-changeableness of His purpose and plan"[2.]*

> *"When people make promises, they guarantee them by appeal to some authority above them so that if there is any question that they'll make good on the promise, the authority will back them up. When God wanted to guarantee his promises, he gave his word, a rock-solid guarantee — God can't break his word. And because his word cannot change, the promise is likewise unchangeable. We who have run for our very lives to God have every reason to grab the promised hope with both hands and never let go. It's an unbreakable spiritual lifeline, reaching past all appearances right to the extraordinary presence of God"*

(Hebrews 6:16-19, The Message)

Harpoon of hope

This constancy is offered as an anchor of my soul. My mind, my will, and my emotions can be held secure and stable by the security of hope in Him, His plan, and purpose for me. This hope is like a lifeline of steel wire bound to a harpoon with counter barbs that cannot be withdrawn or retracted. Once having pierced the veil of Hebrews 6:20 and entered the certainty of His Presence within, such an anchor is secure and unbreakable under the weight of whoever steps upon it.

Whoever.

This is an invitation *to you* to step onto the adequate and strong enough anchor for your drifting and changing mind, emotions, and will. This took me to a place far beyond what I could ever have reached, not only concerning my eternal salvation enabling me to be in the presence of a holy and just God. It also transported me into an enhanced experience and wholeness in this life.

In the Old Testament, there was a rope used to tie around the ministering priest's ankle when he made his annual entrance into the Holy of Holies to atone for the people's sins. The atonement sacrifice was the antecedent of the work of Jesus in presenting Himself on our behalf as a perfect sacrifice acceptable to God. The Old Testament priest had to anticipate the possibility that his sacrifice or presence might be unacceptable to God. Consequently, he could be struck down dead in the secret place. The bells around his garment would cease ringing, and the ministers outside the curtain would know to pull the rope and therefore retrieve the dead priest for burial.

Pulled toward Presence

This New Testament rope is a tensile, lifeline drawing us *into* rather than out of His presence, acceptable, safe and secure!

Hebrews is clear in its adulation of the heroes of faith. They exceeded themselves in overcoming the boundaries of personal comfort and safety as their legacy for all time. Faith gave Sarah physical power (Heb. 11:11).

Their faith controlled and sustained these heroes, even unto death. They acted now as if what they had seen afar off was already theirs. Moses motivated by faith, *gazed upon Him who is invisible!* (Heb. 11:27).

Out of frailty, these heroes won strength, becoming stalwart, even mighty and resistless in battle (Heb.11:34). What an encouragement it is to us that these characters were scourged and, yet, this is not reported as a failure but as growth.

Hebrews 6:10-11 asserts that we must realise and enjoy the full assurance and development of our hope until the end. This is the pursuit of hope rather than sincere and diligent development of ministry. For me, this contrast was a shocking one. How weak and ineffective my efforts had been to develop a foundation from which to minister, despite my best intentions. God was more concerned than anything that *my hope rather than my ministry* would be expanded because this is the key to developing faith.

How I was humbled to discover my misguided efforts to serve God.

Faith is the one thing that divided Jesus' opinion about people

Whether or not they believed, directed Jesus' willingness to get involved. Faith is the one thing that pleases God without which He has no pleasure in us. Faith is a gift, but it is one we must desire, nurture and protect. Faith is the one thing the enemy fears above all else. It is the fuel that ignites our action, witness, and compassion in this life

John 10:10 says that the *only* way you will see God's glory is if you believe. His goodness, his grace, and His presence are released as you expect and hope. And having hope, you trust that what is invisible will become visible and you believe.

"That means that he underwent circumcision as evidence and confirmation of what God had done long before to bring him into this acceptable standing with himself, an act of God he had embraced with his whole life. And it means further that Abraham is the father of all people who embrace what God does for them while they are still on the "outs" with God, as yet unidentified as God's, in an "uncircumcised" condition. It is these people in this condition who are called "set right by God and with God"! Abraham is also, of course, father of those who had undergone the religious rite of circumcision not just because of the ritual but because they were willing to live in the risky faith-embrace of God's action for them, the way Abraham lived long before he was marked by circumcision.

That famous promise God gave Abraham — that he and his children would possess the earth — was not given because of something Abraham did or would do. It was based on God's decision to put everything together for him, which Abraham then entered when he believed. If those who get what God gives them only get it by doing everything they are told to do and filling out all the right forms properly signed that eliminates personal trust and turns the promise into an ironclad contract! That's not a holy promise; that's a business deal. A contract was drawn up by a hard-nosed lawyer and with plenty of fine print only makes sure that you can never collect. But if there is no contract in the first place, simply a promise — and God's promise at that — you can't break it.

This is why the fulfilment of God's promise depends solely on trusting God and his way, and then embracing him and what he does. God's promise arrives as a pure gift. That's the only way everyone can be sure to get in on it, those who keep the religious traditions and those who have never heard of them. For Abraham is the father of us all. He is not our racial father — that's reading the story backwards. He is our faith father.

We call Abraham "father" not because he got God's attention by living like a saint, but because God made something out of Abraham when he was a nobody. Isn't that what we've always read in Scripture, God saying to Abraham, "I set you up as father of many peoples"? Abraham was first named "father" and then became a father because he dared to trust God to do what only God could do: raise the dead to life, with a word make something out of nothing. When everything was hopeless, Abraham believed anyway, deciding to live not because of what he saw he couldn't do but on what God said he would do. And so he was made the father of a multitude of peoples. God himself said to him, "You're going to have a big family, Abraham!"

Abraham didn't focus on his own impotence and say, "It's hopeless. This hundred-year-old body could never father a child." Nor did he survey Sarah's decades of infertility and give up. He didn't tiptoe around God's promise asking sceptical questions. He plunged into the promise and came up strong, ready for God, sure that God would make good on what he had said. That's why it is said, "Abraham was declared fit before God by trusting God to set him right." But it's not just Abraham; it's also us! The same thing gets said about us when we embrace and believe the One who brought Jesus to life when the conditions were equally hopeless. The sacrificed Jesus made us fit for God, set us right with God.

By entering through faith into what God has always wanted to do for us — set us right with him, make *us fit for him — we have it all together with God because of our Master Jesus. And that's not all: We throw open our doors to God and discover at the same moment that he has already thrown open his door to us. We find ourselves standing where we always hoped we might stand — out in the wide open spaces of God's grace and glory, standing tall and shouting our praise.*

There's more to come: We continue to shout our praise even when we're hemmed in with troubles, because we know how troubles can develop passionate patience in us, and how that patience, in turn, forges the tempered steel of virtue, keeping us alert for whatever God will do next. In alert expectancy such as this, we're never left feeling shortchanged. Quite the contrary — we can't round up enough containers to hold everything God generously pours into our lives through the Holy Spirit!"

(Romans 4:11-5:5, The Message)

Clearly, there is a dynamic in the power of expectation and anticipation that we may grossly underestimate. The Bible calls it faith.

CHAPTER 11

A CAPTIVE WORD IS NOT AN EMPTY PROMISE

Afternoon strollers casually linger at the footbridge as the massive gates close upon me once again. Rising waters churn beneath the hold, foam and flecks paint a stark contrast against the deepening black vortex.

Caught in a cauldron of inevitability, I am realising this is just a passing experience, a lesson and a memory that will lend me more in-depth expertise one day in future similar circumstances. I grit my teeth and stare upward at the next inverted beams, water spilling and trickling urgently over the portcullis-like gate walls.

Lock of Promise

First, you *see* what is in your spirit. Then only can you *create* what you have seen there. So, if you feed your faith on the words and thoughts of God, you are creating or bringing the day of His appearing ever more tangibly close.

Many of us live life with certain familiar expectations depending on our upbringing and nationality. As we develop, we are always experiencing the tug of new and better reasons to look forward, *'Christmas is coming'* or *'I can't wait to grow up!'* I remember being told that Father Christmas did not exist. Being one of those rare, naïve children who still believed in him at ten, I was devastated.

I asked, *"Is there anything else?"*

What came next was being told the facts of life.
Gales of laughter followed at the ridiculous prospect of some of my parents' adult friends *'at it'*. I still couldn't help wondering *'Is there anything else?'*

Perhaps it was …
Going to 'big school'?
Getting the key to my own room?
Learning to drive?
Owning my first house?
Getting married?
Having a baby?

These are some of life's greatest joys and to the uninitiated, life's greatest mysteries. But for so many, the next new thing goes sour in our mouth almost as soon as we taste it, perhaps because we try to make it the main thing and expect more of *it* than *it* can deliver.

After this has happened a few times, you can settle for what is "normal", average and predictable so that you can avoid disappointment. The sooner you learn this, the sooner you believe you can protect yourself from false expectation. If you expect little or nothing, then anything else becomes a bonus. Too much Christian experience has been tainted with disappointment and self-protection.

Yet, still you cry,

"Let your mercy and loving-kindness, O Lord, be upon us, in proportion to our waiting and hoping for you"

(Psalm 33:22, NIV)

Great Expectation

This is a dynamic that you can turn to your benefit or allow to your disadvantage. Expectation - or the lack of it can fundamentally sabotage or enable you. When it works against you, you get just as little as you expect. Over-expecting and under-delivering is a fear many are familiar with. And you still can't help wondering,

'Is there anything else?'
All my life I had been wondering *'Is there anything else?'* I could not tolerate the thought that life was just more of the same and then even more again.

God responds to this.

Yes, there is more.

I came to know Jesus Christ as Lord and Saviour, and at last I knew that this 'more' was beyond anything I had imagined.

"I ask him that with both feet planted firmly on love, you'll be able to take in with all Christians the extravagant dimensions of Christ's love. Reach out and experience the breadth! Test its length! Plumb the depths! Rise to the heights! Live full lives, full in the fullness of God. God can do anything, you know — far more than you could ever imagine or guess or request in your wildest dreams! He does it not by pushing us around but by working within us, his Spirit deeply and gently within us"

(Ephesians 3:17-20, The Message)

God-given fulfilment is a gift beyond expectation.

Look at how that felt to the complex character David. It defies definition; defies explanation. He had been on the run from the jealous King Saul, sinned by adultery and murder. He raised dysfunctional children, lost two sons and his deepest friend and confidante by untimely deaths, even feigned madness to save his life. Worst of all, he did not get to build the house of God he had always dreamed of erecting.

Yet, he oozes satisfaction from his spirit as he declares,

> *"Is not my house right with God? Has he not made with me an everlasting covenant, arranged and secured in every part? Will he not bring to fruition my salvation and grant me my every desire?"*

> (2 Samuel 23:5, NIV)

Expectation needs you to come looking for the promises before you can exploit them. It requires you to dare to expect that if God put a spiritual hunger in you, then He will satisfy it with good things. Expecting that there *is* more is brave.

And it's reasonable if the Bible tells you to.

You can expect to receive what has been suggested, revealed, given or accepted. Expectation must be fuelled with faith; a costly commodity. It costs you more than you ever thought you could afford. When it doesn't reveal its fruits, it is still a compulsion.

When you encounter Jesus in the Scriptures, you realise that taking God at His word (and that means knowing it) will lead to amazing results. Authentic expectation is one of the most attractive things about you if you learn to work with it and not against it. You intrigue and attract because you are expectant. You contradict everything people might think holds true about Christians or church.

You exude the compelling belief that something good will happen when you are together.

You expect God.

You expect more. God *does* even more!

When people sense that there is a benefit to them, then *they* too begin to expect.

Anticipating and honouring

That was the expectation of Mary Magdalene who, a few days before the crucifixion, anointed Jesus' feet in anticipation and expectation.

> *"Jesus said, "Let her alone. She's anticipating and honouring the day of my burial"*
>
> (John 12:7, The Message)

Even though she did not understand what would happen because of the death of her loved one, she expected *something* would. The Bible tells us that this quality brings to fulfilment what was always intended.

Isn't that something worth pursuing?

Pregnancy is one of the few waiting games that everyone understands and accepts with relative patience. In fact, there would be a grave concern if anyone tried to accelerate the pregnancy or shortcut the gestation time. From the point of conception, a mother's body becomes an incubator until the new life becomes sustainable. Her waistline must give generously, her energy levels, mobility, and schedule eventually give way entirely for the new life inside them. Isn't it wonderful that the Bible chooses this idea of pregnancy to explain God's heart for us, waiting for the thing that we hope and dream of? He uses the picture of a mother waiting to give birth. Amazingly, he doesn't use an analogy of baking or crafting.

A universal principle

God knew this context of patience and preparation would never go out of date. He wanted us to understand that waiting for an expected future is normal. We all understand the principle of becoming more ready tomorrow for something than today.

> "All around us we observe a pregnant creation. The difficult times of pain throughout the world are simply birth pangs. But it's not only around us; it's within us. The Spirit of God is arousing us within. We're also feeling the birth pangs. These sterile and barren bodies of ours are yearning for full deliverance. That is why waiting does not diminish us, any more than waiting diminishes a pregnant mother. We are enlarged in the waiting. We, of course, don't see what is enlarging us. But the longer we wait, the larger we become, and the more joyful our expectancy"
>
> (Romans 8:22-25, The Message)

Waiting does not diminish us

Waiting is not harmful, disruptive or wasteful, any more than waiting diminishes a pregnant mother. You and I are enlarged in the waiting. And He wants us to know that being altered by this expectation is a good thing. It is an inevitable change that will prepare us to 'give' even more when that thing arrives.

> *"Abraham believed God and it was credited to him as righteousness"*.

> (Romans 4:3 and Genesis 17, NIV)

He had to see that God Himself is determined that His word will come to pass. He would never again have to be tempted that he, and not God, was carrying the promise. He could be freed from having to find the resources and massaging the facts and could know this promise would stand on its own merit. He somehow believed that God was correct in instructing him to sacrifice Isaac.

And that's what Abraham intended to do; to trust in God-righteousness. So, he became righteous. That's also how you stand before God when you trust in Jesus, believing somehow that God's sacrifice of His own son now means you can become righteous. Then you are persuaded. This is enough for you to approach God.

It is my prayer that all of you can be persuaded by the truth and guaranteed security of God's word in your hearts rather than an endless and futile search for intellectual proof or fickle emotional cues.

> *"Then Abraham looked up and glanced around, and behold, behind him was a ram caught in a thicket by his horns. And Abraham went and took the ram and offered it up for a burnt offering and an ascending sacrifice instead of his son!"*

> (Genesis 22: 13-17)

Look up and look around

God wants you to realise that He has already given you everything you need at the point you have arrived, to do whatever he is asking you to do. He wants you to learn to expect to find the answer in your own context and circumstances.

He often knows that you will find the answer in your own heart.

Abraham learned something amazing about what happens when you look up and expect the answer to be in Him. He first looked up, then, he glanced around.

In seeing that God is the Provider, the Jehovah-Jireh[1], he now had a new concept of where everything around him came from. The ram caught in the thicket came from God.

This was the first time God revealed this provisional facet of Himself to anyone.

Caught in advance for you

Now that ram had been caught in the thicket some time ago. I have seen how these animals struggle to free themselves when they are getting left behind. Sheep are not solitary animals, they always follow one another. This one had been left behind some time ago. For three days Abraham hadn't passed the rest of the flock on that side of the mountain. So, this ram had been stuck for a few days. This ram had given up struggling even when Abraham and Isaac came into range. The ram was exhausted, listless and still. We know this because Abraham had to look around to notice it.

It had been there some time. It hadn't caught the attention of the corner of Abraham's eye because it wasn't moving.

Sheep run away when they see humans. If they possibly can, they will. This one was too exhausted to struggle. God had already gone ahead of them some days before to trap this ram in the hedge to serve His purpose through Abraham's obedience rather than his sacrifice.

When you set out in faith, the Word not only does NOT return void, it waits for you *in a future place where you have been told to go.*

A captive word

Another way of thinking about this is that *a captive word is not an empty promise.* A captive word is held somewhere in your future, for the moment that word needs to return to you. First, you must expect that God above has put it there in advance for you. You must go there expecting to encounter it, and when you get there you must look around for it.

Like Abraham, you might even pass it by if you don't first realise God is your source. It will be released on your arrival when you are within sight of it. Jesus was indeed your captive ram that substituted the cost of the price you should really pay. He is not far away.

He is still waiting for you, even if you walked past Him without realising. God,

> "declared [the future] and have saved [the nation in times of danger], and I have shown [that I am God] when there was no strange and alien god among you"

> (Isaiah 43:12-13, AMPC)

> "Whenever you have thrown away your idols, I have shown you my power. With one word I have saved you. You have seen me do it; you are my witnesses

that it is true. From eternity to eternity I am God. No one can oppose what I do."

(Isaiah 43:12-13, TLB)

Only Abraham knew God as *the Father* and is called *father* in the Bible. Only those who know God as the Father (in their dependency) can really be a father. And until a man understands fatherhood, he cannot expect to have true sons. Are you one who expects to reproduce? If you do, you will sow your seed of faith and expectation into the right soil.

A bird in the hand is worth two in the bush

The proverbial birds in the bush are free to fly away at the slightest start which is why the caught bird is so much more valuable. But the Word of God to your life is much more valuable when you let it go. It is of infinite value when you send it out to do the work it is designed for.

You can trust. Whether that bird or word alights on a bush or flies away, it is still yours. It is destined to fulfil what you released it to do.

Do you struggle to believe that the thing God said will happen *will not* return void?

How might it look if it returned void?
How would you be so sure it was void?
If it seems to return void could this be as much about your rejection of it as false or as weak? (Too weak to do what it was supposed to do?)

Or might it return camouflaged, obscure and difficult to recognise it for what it is; a word fulfilled?
How can you be so sure it is time to be discouraged?

Why would you reject what God said and fail to apply confidence in a word you once received?

You have an incredible power to fulfil or disrupt the destiny spoken or written over your life.

Yes, the union of your call and destiny is the consummation of your faith. This is the salvation of your soul. Your mind becomes the mind of Christ. Your emotions are subject to Him and your decisions are made according to His will. That will, His revealed will is called the Word.

The period between a spoken word and its fulfilment is a mysterious and even emotive time. For instance, God moves upon a sceptic even though he is not yet alive to Him. At some point, he is given the gift of the Holy Spirit, that he may have the capacity to become a faith-filled believer.

Like you, he must believe to be able to receive. Not just once but by the continuous acceptance of God's new truths. He promises. You believe. He shows principles that He wants to reveal to you.

For the believer and unbeliever alike, God's word is a liberating and life-giving word.

It brings access and maximum return on everything your life can be as you implement its power by speaking it aloud.

> *"As the rain and the snow come down from heaven, and do not return to it without watering the earth and making it bud and flourish, so that it yields seed for the sower and bread for the eater, so is my word that goes out from my mouth: It will not return to me empty, but will accomplish what I desire and achieve the purpose for which I sent it"*

> (Isaiah 55:10-11, NIV)

The word is sent to accomplish something in your life whether you are uncertain, a person that needs new faith in God, or a believer who is already exercising a certain measure of faith. Therefore, Christians meet to hear the spoken word of God corporately. You are giving Him access to speak; you are giving God fertile ground.

So, faith is not just your first decision for Him. God loves a growing faith that is built upon every ensuing word and causes you to move to action. He values every single inch that you move toward Him. If Isaiah says God's word does not return void, then it must always return with *something*.

It must return with the thing it was sent for!

The Word did not return void

Dare I say it, though? This God, in whom you believe, has often said things you have not actually believed.

Examples of the trustworthiness of God's directive word are peppered throughout the Bible. David returned from battles *with the loot*. Note that he went to battle on the Lord's direction[2]. The Word did not return void for him.

Elijah returned from the desert with fresh confidence and power; the Word did not return void.

Jesus, the Living Word brought all things together from where they were to where they are destined to be.

Jesus came back from death having taken authority over it. He collected up *for us* and ascended *with all* the gifts and graces that we all need to live effectively as ministers of reconciliation.

Jesus, the Word did not return void.

"He climbed the high mountain, He captured the enemy and seized the booty, He handed it all out in gifts to the people. It's true, is it not, that the One who climbed up also climbed down, down to the valley of the earth? And the One who climbed down is the One who climbed back up, up to highest heaven. He handed out gifts above and below, filled heaven with his gifts, filled the earth with his gifts. He handed out gifts of apostle, prophet, evangelist, and pastor-teacher to train Christians in skilled servant work, working within Christ's body, the church, until we're all moving rhythmically and easily with each other, efficient and graceful in response to God's Son, fully mature adults, fully developed within and without, fully alive like Christ."

(Ephesians 4:8-13, The Message)

"God is not a man, that he should lie, nor a son of man, that he should change his mind. Does he speak and then not act? Does he promise and not fulfil? I have received a command to bless; he has blessed, and I cannot change it."

(Numbers 23:19-20, NIV)

"God did this so that, by two unchangeable things in which it is impossible for God to lie, we who have fled to take hold of the hope offered to us may be greatly encouraged".

(Hebrews 6:18, NIV)

Does God's word ever return void?

Does it accomplish that which God desires? 'Yes'.
Has every word of God been accomplished? (Truthfully) 'No'.

Has the word returned void? 'No', 'Well not yet', (more hesitantly now). 'I don't know'.

So where is it then? Where has the word, sent to bless and release and to favour you, gone? Is it lost in the eternal ether? Is your hope departed?

No'. Absolutely and emphatically not.

He is not a liar. The word has not returned void, and because it has not returned then it must be held up somewhere, held for you, even. Until such a time as it can be returned.

Take heart, it has merely not returned yet.

Time is the confounding factor that our faith must contend with. Yes, there is often a delay. Sometimes short and sometimes long. Nevertheless, God's word stands true, and it will not be found false.

Do you remember the lyrics of the folk song?
        "where have all the flowers gone, long time passing?"[3]

Maybe you would sing?
        "Where has all the promise gone, long time passing?"

A lock or a logjam

Maybe your promise is caught in an apparent lock-down in the intended progress of your barge. Maybe there is a blockage in the waterway you sail. The usual passage allowing the word to return fruitful has closed. The attached blessing is caught in a narrow pound, sealed in by a lock or a logjam of debris where it cannot work out its purpose and fulfilment for you.

God's word can travel through many inconvenient and frustrating locks. Then there are also the stretches of experience that you spend between the necessary locks of acceptance, hope, expectation, faith, and trust. These are the flat stretches of water called pounds.

These are the long-term seasons or tests in-between each elevation in life, such as

The Pound of Fear

The Pound of Disobedience

The Pound of Containment

The Pound of Irrelevance

The Pound of Carelessness

And ultimately the Pound of Rejection

You cannot afford to reject the Word of God.
Its return, its homecoming is guaranteed. Remember, it may merely be delayed.

Perhaps your word has not returned but neither has it returned void. It has not failed, but it cannot return until the channel is unblocked or the lock gate is opened for access to the full promise of God over your life. The right action must be taken. Sometimes that action is just to wait until the water table of your faith is raised to the next level.

The word will not return void, it simply *will not return until* it can bring home everything it was destined to bring you. It lays dormant but incorruptible. It cannot rot or perish or its power decay, unlike the rubbish that chokes it.

It will outlast the frustration.

When are you going to realise the power of this watercourse - the canal of life, once relieved of its rubble and weeds? Incredible things can happen when you start this conservation work of nurture and extraction of the word that was sent on a mission into your life.

Don't stop expecting

Realise that there is a way to regain everything that God said. It is liberating. *Not to expect* God to bail out or prise you out of your congestion; that is unfair.

Is this your wheedling cry? *"I'm a Christian, get me out of here!"* No, God gives a word, a vision, a dream or a hope that He expects *you* to believe for.

One summer

I had a powerful insight from God about expectation.

I was visiting a beautiful place near my sister's home, in the Welsh Elan Valley. I stood at the top of the dam overlooking the expanse of water on the one side and the steep wall on the other. The valley is now flooded by a river diverted from its original course where a large dam to contain it was finished in 1952. Elan Vale was submerged so the river could take its new course to harness the power and resource of the accumulated water.

Even a church building was submerged in the interest of the project.

The newly created reservoir became a water supply for Birmingham Corporation. To supply water to the distant city, an extensive system of pipework had to be laid. The project was hailed as a remarkable feat of engineering and took many years to complete. It was ahead of its time. No one could have predicted then, the demand today upon its water supply.

The construction comprised the structure of the dam itself but also integral to that, a system of turbines and generators that would harness the flow of the water and convert it into electricity. It is still performing adequately today despite the massive rise in the population of Birmingham. There has been a continuous supply of water for the metropolis and a local source of electricity for the towns and villages of the surrounding Valleys.

In the exhibition centre at Elan Valley was one of those interactive museum models that demonstrated the mechanism of water-flow and energy conversion into electricity.

I watched a few people pumping a handle with some effort to transport water up a pipe and into a cistern. When the volume reached a critical point, a lever was activated, and water flowed through an outflow pipe and caused a turbine to generate enough power to light a light bulb.

Wowed amazement lit the faces of the children who tried it. I too had a go. I stood back to watch the water flowing down the pipe and switch on the light temporarily.

Then God showed me something amazing. He said this to my imagination.

Why have you stopped pumping?

Because I stopped (perhaps because you stopped) only a limited supply of water pumped into the pipe and therefore the light bulb was extinguished. Everyone came to this demonstration, operated and understood a principle at work, then went away again.

The next person had to create a brand-new head of pressure all over again.

I ask a question of us all, "Why don't you begin pumping and when the spectacle begins, *keep pumping* so the light will continue to shine even while you marvel at it?"

God spoke so clearly to me in that place, once touched by a mighty revival outpouring in 1904-5[4].

Why did revival stop then?

It stopped because somebody stopped pumping. It stopped because the people were so touched by the miracle, so amazed by the love of God and the healings and the supernatural manifestations that they stopped to marvel and forgot to tend to the things of God. I am not saying they sinned, or that they were casual about what they experienced for indeed their worst fear was that the presence of God would move and lift.

You and I can learn from this, to continue to apply all that we have been taught and know is true. It teaches us,

- to expect the extraordinary even when everything is ordinary.
- that when the extraordinary unfolds, we must not neglect the ordinary. *Even amid of the extraordinary, the ordinary must continue.*

You must expect, and you must continue to expect even when that which you are seeking begins to be manifested.

"the glorious riches of this mystery, which is Christ in you, the hope of glory"

(Colossians 1:27, NIV)

The hope of glory will be increasingly revealed IN YOU.

How do you think this will happen if it is not in the ordinary contacts and interactions you have with the people you live and move around? God wants you to expect and believe for a flow of influence that exceeds what seems necessary or realistic. He allows Himself to be limited both by the scale of what you expect and by the discontinuity of your expectation.

Remember the wise and foolish virgins of the parable about the Lord's return?

Like the two types described, you may expect and then sit back, or you can expect *and* continue to expect. You can fill your oil lamps or fill your lamps and carry some more oil in case expectation is outlasted or exceeded.

"From the west, men will fear the name of the LORD, and from the rising of the sun, they will revere his glory. For he will come like a pent-up flood that the breath of the LORD drives along"

(Isaiah 59:19, NIV)

You know from the scriptures. Sometimes you might not receive much warning. He will come like a thief in the night. In the event of 'it' happening there will not be any point *then* to start expecting.

In nature, flash floods continue to take communities by surprise, or villages fall prey to monsoons.

Flooding occurs for various reasons

- Because there is an inadequate flood defence to protect the land from possible submersion such as the 2005 devastation to New Orleans caused by Hurricane Katrina[4].

- Because the inevitable event is not prevented or prepared for, as caused by the recurring monsoons of Bangladesh.

- Because the freak circumstances leading to it are unique to a time and space and the risk of flood is exceptional (such as the 2004 flash floods of Boscastle, UK[5]).

- Because gulleys and drains capable of draining excess water have become blocked, as in Toll Bar of my own Doncaster borough[6] (2007).

A lack of preparation may be complacency in ignoring the *expected* flood. Or an *unexpected* flood defying the usual trends of weather and geography means a community is taken off-guard. In either case, there is a trail of havoc and destruction wrought upon the land and livestock. There are lives lost and changed forever.

These natural phenomena demonstrate a spiritual principle.

Without expectation, you fail to actively and purposefully prepare and prevent.

While you are ignorant or complacent, an awful lot of people lose destinies, miss opportunities and have disrupted life histories.

They are swept away without the chance to begin expecting themselves.

You must build with expectation, maintain the drains and prepare a dam that will be able to channel the flow of God's Spirit into your area. You should think big because God does. You should be careful to have pipes laid into all the areas of life that God calls you to so that living water will flow there, unpolluted and fresh. You should install turbines that will harness the power of the Spirit so that the Light of the world may be seen by many and for as long as there is water because of your good deeds.

> *"You are the light of the world. A city on a hill cannot be hidden. Neither do people light a lamp and put it under a bowl. Instead, they put it on its stand, and it gives light to everyone in the house. In the same way, let your light shine before men, that they may see your good deeds and praise your Father in heaven"*

> (Matthew 5:14-16, NIV)

The ultimate outcome can be better. Far beyond all your hopes and dreams and expectations than even the good you hang onto. There *is coming* an upsurge of a spiritual tide of life and it will well up from within each one of you and will be inescapable for everyone around. The scale and power of the life that is already within you will become increasingly evident to the world.

May you be found ready so that the flood of favour and fruitfulness you believe for becomes an inheritance. It will not just be another interactive demonstration. It will be real; your long-term rule and reign as kings and priests with influence and favour. You will be the church glorified whom He will return for!

It will happen quickly.
It will not fall out of the sky.
It will begin in you and through you.

This flood is the groundswell of the expectation which is in us.

An invisible dam

You will not be able to *contain* Him, but the fact you are ready to receive Him is the reason He will come. When you build this dam of expectation, the water that is already there merely accumulates in a different way, a way that is dramatically effective. The faith of Joshua whose toes entered the Jordan caused the water of the river to accumulate in a different way, piling in a heap upstream at Adam.

Matthew Henry called this an invisible dam[7].

You too are invisible dams, delicately holding Him in expectation, as you allow His Spirit to speak to you,

"Now", "No", "Yes", "Flow", "Hold back", "Shine", and *"Release"*

CHAPTER 12
FAITH STARTS AT SUNSET

Contrary to all previous plans and preparations, I succumb to the draining heat of late afternoon as the sun's rays pin me to a temporary resting place in the bow. I sit back against a pile of fraying rope and brittle tarpaulin. I weakly wrestle with impinging thoughts of unseen dangers but the persuasive balm of heat and brilliant light bleach out these protestations. Colour drains from the fiercely baking hedgerows and verdant hills.

My aching limbs and frame settle with surprise at their cradling, intimate support and I play private games, entertaining imaginary psychedelic images on the inner screens of my eyelids. We are moving without effort, buoyed again by the opening submerged sluices. Glittering waters boil like jam as Lock keeper waits for the setting point to pour us into the final pound.

The Lock of Faith

Remember that *Jesus answered,*

> *"Are there not twelve hours of daylight? A man who walks by day will not stumble, for he sees by this world's light. It is when he walks by night that he stumbles, for he has no light".*

(John 11:9-10, NIV)

They say that the darkest hour is before the dawn.

Many of our finest moments are borne from pressure, struggle and resistance. Inexplicable darkness setting in on the sunset of a bright success, brings a transient, powerful and colourful sustaining vision of the world. In the face of the coming dark night of the soul, you reassure yourself of another inevitable cycle of light returning to repeat itself. There is something refreshing and hopeful about the emerging dawn of a new day. It can bring relief, herald significance or simply re-calibrate our diurnal nature. Here is another threshold of beginning, a renewed application, a new insight, even a sudden understanding and perspective.

The lonely pursuit of an obscure path

Critical seasons of change are often accompanied by the lonely pursuit of an obscure path. Called the dark night of the soul, it has become accepted as a universally acknowledged experience of spiritual growth. The 'dark night' could be a letting go of your own understanding of who you are, inviting change that can bring about a complete transformation of your way of defining self and your relationship to God.

The transition can be isolating, incomprehensible, and even desolating. During the 'dark night' one who has developed a strong consistent discipline in devotion to God, suddenly finds their relationship with Him difficult and unrewarding for an extended period. God may seem to have abandoned them, or their prayers hit the ceiling, bouncing back unheard.

Yet, choosing to apply faith as a principle is not as mystical as it might seem. You apply a certain measure of faith to many aspects of your life with regularity and ease. You wait patiently for the bus **as if** it were going to arrive. You pay your holiday deposits **as if** the travel company would stay in business. You teach and invest in your kids **as if** they will need those skills in later life.

Increasingly, I wanted to live **as if** everything God had said were true and would come true. I wanted to know a deepening and confident relationship with Him that would transform the way I looked at life and circumstances. So that even if there were circumstances I did not comprehend, I could still love the skin I was in because I could look at myself and my situation through God's eyes.

> *"I keep asking that the God of our Lord Jesus Christ, the glorious Father, may give you the Spirit of wisdom and revelation, so that you may know him better. I pray also that the eyes of your heart may be enlightened in order that you may know the hope to which he has called you, the riches of his glorious inheritance in the saints, and his incomparably great power for us who believe"*

> (Ephesians 1:17-19, NIV)

God sees things so differently from us and that is why we need to have the eyes of our heart enlightened by the spirit of wisdom and revelation. And years ago, God gave me great insight into the way he sees us compared to the incomplete way we view ourselves.

This insight into the 'walk of faith' downloaded into my spirit on a commute from a seminar in my previous city of residence. This was just the beginning of a lead up to the larger transformation of faith that took place as I stepped into full-time ministry some seven years later. In fact, it was the conception of the revelation that is this message of 'As If' today.

> "Once returning home from Hull at dusk, crossing the canal at the M18 flyover, I saw to my left, a barge sailing into the darkness, pushing into the choppy water. To my right, there was a large golden sun, silhouetting the trees and picking out a trailing golden ribbon of reflected light that streaked towards me. There I was, on the motorway looking from the same position at the same canal, only half of which was brilliantly illuminated by the sun. I realised that God is with us in our experience and position AND simultaneously stands in His finished and completed position in heaven. He looks at the same thing I look at but from a different perspective! God sees everything from completion".

(Journal entry)[1]

He is.

He says His name is I AM. He was there at your conception and He knew then how everything turns out. He looks back at your whole life and sees a golden ribbon of light.[1]

> "The path of the righteous is like the first gleam of dawn, shining ever brighter till the full light of day"

(Proverbs 4:18, NIV)

You can't always see (it) because you're not viewing things as God does.

"Now faith is being sure of what we hope for and certain of what we do not see"

(Hebrews 11:1, NIV)

You see dark choppy water all the way ahead, but from where He's standing its brilliant, all the way to completion. Viewed from God's perspective, what might have seemed a delusion seems a little easier, a believable destiny even? From where God stands, way up on the horizon where you are heading, He looks back along with all the saints and cheers you on from the place that His light reflects upon your whole life.

"The ways of right-living people glow with light; the longer they live, the brighter they shine. But the road of wrongdoing gets darker and darker — travellers can't see a thing; they fall flat on their faces"

(Proverbs 4:18-19, The Message)

As if you have hindsight

God knows His light has touched your whole life and streaks across your whole destiny toward the final goal. He sees that it is done, but you also must view things with His hindsight as if you are already there looking back. Faith is viewing events as if you have hindsight when you only have foresight. Your (faith) foresight is effective when it is created through your eyes of God's hindsight-enlightened hearts.

As I keep repeating,

"[For I always pray to] the God of our Lord Jesus Christ, the Father of glory, that he may grant you a spirit of wisdom and revelation [of insight into mysteries and secrets] in the [deep and intimate] knowledge

of Him, By having the eyes of your heart flooded with light, so that you can know and understand the hope to which He has called you, and how rich is his glorious inheritance in the saints (His set apart ones), And [so that you can know and understand] what is the immeasurable and unlimited and surpassing greatness of His power in and for us who believe, as demonstrated in the working of his mighty strength,"

(Ephesians 1:17-19)

If faith is a struggle, ask how much has your heart been enlightened? If you know God, you will know what He desires, and your desires will be His. Let me ask you this question,

"What do you sincerely desire or hope for?"

Do you view this positively, even *as if* it will happen? Or, do you say scornfully to yourself or even God *"Yeah, As if!"*.

Without inner conviction of the perspective of God you are merely enjoying a fantasy.

To act out, confess, or even pretend that you believe you will receive the object of your faith is folly. Without this total assurance, you do not have faith. Without it, you cannot hope to enter the destiny written into the book of your life, but you remain deluded. Even if they are laudable delusions, without the fuel of faith, they are vapour-like delusions.

One is faith - one is fantasy!

The great news is that faith is a gift and that it can simply be received by understanding that it is a gift. You must stand at the place of fulfilment.

You stop being the obstacle between the call and the destiny, the source and the outflow.

Standing on the circumstances between God and the future, casts a shadow over it, making it more fearful and intimidating. Yet, you want to make it. You hope you will make it. That's a godly desire isn't it? And *you do* stand between where God created you and where He wants you to go. You are somewhere in between these two until your dying day. Paul Scanlon[2] once called it *"Living in the dash"* (that is the hyphen representing your whole life between your birth day and date of death.)

So, how can you learn to live with the weight of an unknown future without it casting a shadow of fear, doubt or confusion over you?

If you are going to *'make it'* where should you stand?

All the great faith preachers claim that you should be 'standing on the word'. You stop standing on the intermediate circumstances and see that you have already entered His throne room and are seated with Him. You are ruling and reigning in life because He has given you the permission and capacity to do so!

> *"...we have gained access by faith into this grace in which we now stand. And we rejoice in the hope of the glory of God"*
>
> (Romans 5:2, NIV)

If you stand in His grace, you stand in His finished and perfected work of grace. You are completely acceptable and welcome in His presence. You know that all you need is in Him.

> *"Not only so, but we also rejoice in our sufferings, because we know that suffering produces*

perseverance; perseverance, character; and character, hope. And hope does not disappoint us, because God has poured out his love into our hearts by the Holy Spirit, whom he has given us."

(Romans 5:3-5, NIV)

Sometimes you fear that expecting too much will leave you disappointed.

"Hope deferred makes the heart sick, but a longing fulfilled is a tree of life"

(Proverbs 13:12, NIV).

Disappointment happens when you expect the wrong things when those things are not based upon truth. God says it is OK to check out the facts and enquire after the integrity of what has been offered. In fact, that is the lifelong study of Him; to seek Him and His ways, which will never, never disappoint you. When you know Him, you will have the right desires and will trust even in *the dash.*

Live life more brightly

If you are going to live life more brightly, how should you stand? You must know what He has said and what you must do and that if *He* said it, it will be fulfilled in Him, from Him, for Him and to Him!

"And of this gospel I was appointed a herald and an apostle and a teacher. That is why I am suffering as I am. Yet I am not ashamed, because I know whom I have believed, and am convinced that he is able to guard what I have entrusted to him for that day"

(2 Timothy 1:11-12, NIV)

Oh, to live **as if** everything God said is true, already fulfilled and yet to be realised, **as if** the word (that seems to be captive) is not an empty promise. To live **as if** God is not a liar. Then you must be acquainted with Him or you will wrongly attribute to Him your resultant frustration and disappointment.

> *"In alert expectancy such as this, we're never left feeling short-changed"*

(Romans 5:5, The Message)

You rest in God by grace, through faith, already in a place that you will reach one day. Your heart catches a glimpse of that and gives you in advance, the hindsight necessary for you to finish the course.

Even though the sun may be behind you!
Even though the waterway ahead is darkening and gloomy, a rainbow is developing in the sky above. God is gracious to give a sign of His promise being true. He wants you to live **as if** you have received everything He promised because you have. It has all been given, not earned!

This is your life work — believing

This is your glory, the glory of His light that rises upon you. God asks that in faith, you see yourselves at the end of that journey. The narrowboat has arrived. It is not a shadow - casting obstruction between the light and its destination. What you find is that, even if the world goes dark, the light that disappeared behind you like the setting sun, will arise before you.

Just as certainly as it disappeared, the new day will come. You see that He is outside of time and space and your own understanding. He works patiently with you at the pace you determine for the coming of the fullness to maturity of the times. He enables you in your preparation as the Bride of Christ, the church of God, for your long-anticipated day of consummation.

CHAPTER 13
HE RETURNS WHEN YOU REST

Darkening hedgerows become sharply defined against now turquoise skies. With morose cows and dancing midges for company, we hug the banks of our dictated course. We proceed to the next lock. Having embarked upon the staircase we must continue to the fifth stage despite the lengthening shadows. A tungsten heaven glowers at the metallic water surface, the heavy scent of meadowsweet hanging in the damp evening air. This time I approach the last lock of the staircase. Fear that gave way to anxiety now slides into a largely comforting belief that even in the fading light we are in safe hands.

The Lock of Trust

"Let him who walks in the dark, who has no light, trust in the name of the LORD and rely on his God,"

(Isaiah 50:10, NIV)

Everything you need for life and godliness

My season of faith began to settle into a broad and simple sense of liberating security. I was able to start resting in the fact that God knew what He was doing, where He was taking me and how to get there. He also knew who I would need to meet along the way, especially if they themselves would be instrumental in getting me further. He knew when it would be vital that I could assist in getting them there too. In the process I would find all the necessary knowledge,

"too wonderful for me, too lofty for me to attain"

(Psalm 139:6, NIV)

This knowledge and certainty were beginning to unfold my destiny, and a lived reality of God's Sovereign Presence, power and provision. These were all aspects I had never grasped before. I had lost myself but found myself in Him. During catastrophic alienation, I found an intimacy that had eluded me. In the place of failure, I found the healing of being and not doing. I found the paradox of gaining through losing to enter and be in a place I need not have feared.

In this place David had also meditated on his God and my God.

"To you, O LORD, I lift up my soul; in you I trust, O my God. Do not let me be put to shame, nor let my enemies triumph over me.
No-one whose hope is in you will ever be put to shame, but they will be put to shame who are treacherous without excuse.
Show me your ways, O LORD, teach me your paths; guide me in your truth and teach me, for you are God my Saviour, and my hope is in you all day long.
Remember, O LORD, your great mercy and love, for they are from of old.

Remember not the sins of my youth and my rebellious ways; according to your love remember me, for you are good, O LORD.

Good and upright is the LORD; therefore he instructs sinners in his ways.

He guides the humble in what is right and teaches them his way.

All the ways of the LORD are loving and faithful for those who keep the demands of his covenant.

For the sake of your name, O LORD, forgive my iniquity, though it is great.

Who, then, is the man that fears the LORD? He will instruct him in the way chosen for him.

He will spend his days in prosperity, and his descendants will inherit the land.

The LORD confides in those who fear him; he makes his covenant known to them.

My eyes are ever on the LORD, for only he will release my feet from the snare.

Turn to me and be gracious to me, for I am lonely and afflicted.

The troubles of my heart have multiplied; free me from my anguish

Look upon my affliction and my distress and take away all my sins.

See how my enemies have increased and how fiercely they hate me!

Guard my life and rescue me; let me not be put to shame, for I take refuge in you.

May integrity and uprightness protect me, because my hope is in you".

(Psalm 25, NIV)

As the last lock of the five-rise staircase loomed ahead, I realised these fundamental appeals of David were questions I had not faced before with any honesty.

Did I believe that God is who He says he is? (Yes, I did).
Did I believe that the Bible is God's Word? (Yes, I did).
Did I believe that the Word is a lamp to my feet and a light
to my path? (Er, yes).
Was God a liar? (No, but I couldn't understand His methods).

God's ways are always higher than ours.

Spinning wheel

As a girl I often walked, to my Grandma Kearsley's local Denehurst park in Rochdale. She used to tell my sister and me to stay off the merry-go-round when the big boys were there. In case they sent it spinning too fast. They were renowned for carelessly teasing or frightening off the smaller children from the carousel - pulling it so vigorously no one dared to move. Soon we worked out that if we sat on the very top of the central hub of the centrifuge, it was much safer and much less likely to throw us off.

God has created a special place in your whirlwind-like life where you need to get right on top of his knee, into His purposes and provision, His security and strength. Oftentimes you need to venture to the edges of the carousel to play, to explore and then to go home for tea. Living on the edges of what God has told you, at the end of yourselves and sometimes in the grip of fear, is also a place where you can experience the thrill of His Presence. But you also need to know when the best thing is to sit tight on the hub.

The hub is the safest place to be

While you are resting, God is fashioning you for greatness. You are *resting* into a higher level of trust and a place of greater dependency on Him.

A similar principle can be seen in motor acceleration. A friend of mine, a much more skilled driver than I, noticed that I often left my gear one-below its potential. She explained something I should have known many years earlier. Had I been observing the number of revolutions per minute, she told me, I would know exactly when the engine was being overstressed and when I was over-revving.

The engine can work much more efficiently in the right gear. Its RPM dial indicates relative effort and effectiveness. It was an insight for me to realise that even in need of more speed, changing up a gear could decrease the revolutions per minute.

Going up a gear does not necessarily take more effort

Do you work harder than ever and yet feel as though you are grinding to a halt?

I needed to learn to do what was more effective rather than what just made me tired. Though my demand for speed was increasing, the revolutions could be slowing down at the same time. Have you ever seen the spokes of a wheel or the blades of a turbine spinning faster and faster until they suddenly appear to reverse, slow again, stop still and then go forward? The illusion of apparent reverse motion is at work.

Living according to the dictates of the spirit, rather than the flesh, can also play such tricks upon our logical and limited minds.

He can work this in the core of your being. He calls you to slow down. You may worry that you are falling into a reverse situation and, yet, the pace is faster than ever!

And to whom did God swear that they would never enter his rest if not to those who disobeyed? So we see that they were not able to enter, because of their unbelief.

Therefore, since the promise of entering his rest still stands, let us be careful that none of you be found to have fallen short of it. For we also have had the good news proclaimed to us, just as they did; but the message they heard was of no value to them, because they did not share the faith of those who obeyed. Now we who have believed enter that rest, just as God has said,

"So I declared on oath in my anger,

'They shall never enter my rest.'"

And yet his works have been finished since the creation of the world.

(Hebrews 3:18-4:3, NIV)

Who is this people of unbelief that God was referring to?

"they set out from the mountain of the LORD and travelled for three days. The ark of the covenant of the LORD went before them during those three days to find them a place to rest. The cloud of the LORD was over them by day when they set out from the camp. Whenever the ark set out, Moses said, "Rise up, O LORD! May your enemies be scattered; may your foes flee before you." Whenever it came to rest, he said, "Return, O LORD, to the countless thousands of Israel"

(Numbers 10:33-36, NIV)

The Ark of the Covenant was a visual demonstration to the people of Israel that God was in their midst. The Ark represents the leadership of today's church. It was the leaders that carried the Ark. It fascinates me that for God's presence upon the people to return, the leaders had to come to a place of rest and set down the Ark to rest.

When you are at rest, you are not necessarily inactive. Stillness is an activity of choice and priority that attracts the very presence of God. It is an active choice to be still and to trust rather than make something happen according to your own understanding (however enlightened that understanding might seem). Clearly, if you feed your faith on the words of God and continue to rest in His promises, you are bringing the day of His appearing ever closer and ever more tangible.

It is a little like this when you are straining with impatience to receive a long-awaited guest or far flung relative. Within the frame between the time the guest should arrive and the time that they appear, you start to notice things about your house.

You notice stuff that you would never normally see.

Maybe something private was left lying around, or you notice a rubbish bin that needs emptying. You start looking around you with a heightened sense of scrutiny and awareness as you see your home through the eyes of the one that is coming and interpret what is before you with the eyes of one who is not normally around. DVD's are returned to their corresponding cases. Even the recesses of the settee are checked out. The tension can become unbearable. You keep boiling the kettle and watching through the curtains. The slightest disruption is dealt with and order restored to a near perfect state.

God cares about the small details because it is in the ordinary things that you are held accountable to Him. You must have your house in order, your relational accounts with one another kept short and clean. It's through the small things that He will achieve the large. He makes you wait because you need to notice the disarray in the ordinariness of our life. This, (if put right) would speak volumes to those you live with and prepare you for the extraordinary to follow suit.

Everything becomes a laughing matter

Then comes the moment a long-expected guest arrives. Despite all the efforts to attain to a perfectly presented home, soon there is disarray and mess. When your visitor arrives with news and baggage, presents and photos of their new life or their recent trip, suddenly the house is unrecognisable.

A drink gets knocked over in all the excitement and your response is kind and forgiving instead of harsh. It really doesn't matter. New experiences are shared and gifts and refreshments savoured. Everything becomes a laughing matter as you see things through the gracious eyes of your visitor. In other words, it isn't so much the perfection of the order in the house as the fact that you, the host stayed vigilant and ready for your guest.

That is what is so important.

Neither will He come for perfection. He will mess up any idea you may have of what He is going to do. When He comes, you will not contain Him, and the fact you are ready and waiting to receive Him is the only reason He will come.

This is how it has got to be as you wait; as you strain forward toward the goal.

To be found ready.

Waiting is not passive, it's active and diligent.

God will teach you the lesson of indefinite expectation. You begin to experience such rest as,

- His spiritual and financial favour.

- His connection and influence.

- His success and ability.

Cultivate a state of restful expectation; it matters so much more than a state of perfect readiness. It's your trust and expectancy that He fills rather than perfection. So how can you rest without becoming bored, frustrated or even fearful and frantic?

> *"Teach us to number our days aright, that we may gain a heart of wisdom"*

> (Psalm 90, NIV)

If only you will relinquish your unknown future into the hands of an all-knowing God. If you can abandon all illusion of mastery and control to the powerful, silent process called *trust,* He will teach you who you really are.

In the process you become so much more prepared, more able to appreciate, to be your real authentic self. All because you start to see yourself as He sees you. He sees you through eyes of Love and forgiveness. This is an incredibly healing revelation.

His apparent delays and frustration are evidence of His love.

The act of preparation and readiness is for your sake that your attitude may be proved. And now in turn you can be trusted to speak of His Love with the right motive and indebtedness to Him.

Out of freedom we respond with our work

As *do-er* of my generation, to learn to rest in an achievement driven society was not the easiest lesson of my life. But it was the most profoundly important. I *craved* peace but had no idea how to reach it unless I had first worked through the long list of things to do. I took decades to realise that I would never get to the bottom of that list. By the time I discovered principle-centred guide books, I was already too far gone. Dawn[1] argues the Biblical basis for a weekly whole day's Sabbath rest (especially for pastors and church staff). Instead of *"working our heads off to gain some days of holiday, we rest first and then, out of the Joy of that rest, work for the next six days. Grace reclaims us first, and out of its freedom we respond with our work."*

The Sabbath begins at sunset rather than upon awakening. Its preliminary experience then is of darkness, silence and supposed rest.

Adam's first day, the seventh day of creation, was the Sabbath. He started his first day of life resting, equipping him for the ordained work ahead. Applying this pattern to your frenzied lifestyles would be to regard the gift of time with the gratitude intended. Having faith that you have the time to do what you are intended to, you can follow God's call. You can discern just what that call is. Practising rest is to practise consistently and make perfect a discipline that bolsters confidence in being simply loved and not for what you can accomplish. So, in seasons of God's 'stopping' of momentum in your lives, you can embrace His will because you have learned to anticipate its secret delights through chosen habits of rest.

Static seasons

It may have been a default result rather than a conscious decision to be jammed in a static place in life. No one chooses to become bored, to become frustrated. However, it is always a conscious and active decision to rest or to take stock to re-set your course. Everyone needs maps and signposts, guides and directions. Your clarity is crucial. You could even become God's Lock-keeper and stand in for others, at what may be their gap between progress and stagnation.

You know that it is easy to take a wrong turn, through indecision, ignorance or willful-ness. Even so, your faith; rather your trust, is now the convincing testimony. Your trust is the signpost that it pays to believe the Word, to stay on the waterway and not become daunted or impatient.

When your testimonies are ambiguous and not authentic, it's as if you are sabotaging the rules of the waterway. Frantically battering on the solid wood doors, leaving locks open or opening them before the paddles are released: these actions are careless, selfish and even dangerous. They are a potentially deadly and damaging example.

Rather, as God's guide, standing at these junctions in the flow of life, you can offer others your own powerful testimony. As a result, *their* word will not become void or choked in a backwater of poor decision making or undisciplined living.

Like Abraham's ram, their promised word may just need some help to disentangle.

So, reclaim your promises and theirs, and see the fruition of them in your life.

You see, a captive word is not an empty promise.

It is a fulfilled promise awaiting its timely release.

LIMPING - BRIDGE

YOU DECLARE "AS IF"!

After Jacob returned from Paddan Aram, God appeared to him again and blessed him. God said to him, "Your name is Jacob, but you will no longer be called Jacob; your name will be Israel." So he named him Israel.

And God said to him, "I am God Almighty; be fruitful and increase in number. A nation and a community of nations will come from you, and kings will come from your body. The land I gave to Abraham and Isaac I also give to you, and I will give this land to your descendants after you." Then God went up from him at the place where he had talked with him.

Jacob set up a stone pillar at the place where God had talked with him, and he poured out a drink offering on it; he also poured oil on it. Jacob called the place where God had talked with him Bethel.

Then they moved on from Bethel.

(Genesis 35:9–16, NIV)

Legacy; the reclaimed promise

Sometime long after dark, we ate a simple evening supper of scrambled eggs on toast.

When I was a teen, this was a recipe my own father used to carefully cook to what he considered to be the right gelatinous consistency. Hot melted butter (considered risky in those days) solidified the gently fork-whipped whites and yolks into curds with pepper, salt, nutmeg and herbs. It pleased me to see my granddaughter preparing this for Trea, four generations later.

Still smarting from the loss of her childhood 'comfort blanket' this evening, Trea was subdued and hopeful her mother would not notice the missing dragon. As Swan gently piled the creamy eggs onto our plates, Trea and I exchanged a darting look and seemed to know that we had an explanation to prepare that would satisfy Swan's understanding.

Future hope replaces lost comfort

This was the opportunity to introduce the bracelet.

Yes, I felt it to be the right moment.

Trea's petulant outburst had cost her dearly. She showed the same reluctance to rely upon inspired wisdom but rather trust her own best efforts. This trait had been my own lengthy undoing (just as Jacob had wasted the years of his prime due to his own flawed character).

I told Trea a simple version of the story of *My Secret Name*[1]. Her eyes widened as she heard me tell of my natural mischief and playfulness that drowned in responsibility and self-consciousness, as I lost myself somewhere on life's route. She puzzled at my tale of creeping fear and frustration instead of celebrating uniqueness and distinction. I cautioned her about the constraints of comparison and peer pressure, inhibition or self-doubt, *whatever* the personal and prevalent threat was called that tried to label and dictate to her.

I encouraged her to seek and embrace and then live to fulfil her own secret name, one personally given of God. Here is an extract from my diary, (28th January 2002).

> *A name seems such an arbitrary thing that we have not even chosen - how could we say that we are what we are called – BUT the Old Testament is a pattern of the accuracy with which God knows and calls and has names us. We have a new name written in Heaven that is the epitome of our calling and destiny. It is what we will be known by! Let it be known before we even get there, so our identity will be akin to the name written in heaven!*
>
> *(Revelation 3:12 and 2 Samuel 5:7,12).*

My imparting of this revelation to Trea had come much earlier than expected, but I knew that now she was receptive to the beauty of this moment.

After her mother had kissed Trea goodnight, I slipped into her room and perched on the divan. Gingerly opening a hinged leather-bound gift box, I pushed open the crackly tissue to reveal a stunning three-quarter circlet gold band, not quite a whole circle for ease of removing from the wrist. It had always been in the family since it was bought prophetically for the woman my baby daughter Esme would become. Esme's paternal grandmother Roopea purchased the expensive present for my firstborn with a government disability grant she saved during her time in UK residence. Esme had inherited it upon her eighteenth birthday long after Roopea's death. Now it belonged to Swan and still did, but tonight Trea would see it for herself and know that it was to be hers one day.

I lifted the fine gold band so that Trea could see the meandering decoration like an aerial watercourse that stopped and then spiralled; coiled at the end like a mooring rope. Two fishes darted toward the other end of the bracelet in what looked like a sealed compartment of lock gates also inhabited by a snake like intruder. It was an artistic representation of life's course and challenges; delicate, beautiful, mysterious and valuable.

Too large to be secure on Trea's narrow wrist, she knew it would be many years before she would be trusted to wear it, but it gave her a precious glimpse of a horizon she would reach one day. She gazed longingly and in awed silence for some moments and without being asked, then slipped it off and nestled it back in its paper shroud before peeping one last time at the "fish end".

Jacob had grasped his inheritance too soon, I had striven for mine. And all along, if we had only known, God had been with us in this place, in the first place and we hadn't known it.

I wanted Trea to know the power of trusting, patiently waiting *now* for the right timing of this inheritance in her life.

All along our journey, *in* the narrowboat, you too are *in* the place all these things you desire have already been provided.

CHAPTER 14
TAKE YOUR STAND

Exiting from beneath its leafy canopy into the aqueduct, the narrowboat sails into open view. From the air, she is a gleaming red pencil floating in a trough. From the elevated towpath, she glides beside pedestrians who find the steep elevation unnerving. A grand imposing design and feat of architectural audacity, the canal straddles the valley on her domino-spaced row of heavy stone pillars

We sail amongst the swooping martins and seem to be able to reach and touch the crystal plane trails; confusing and conflicting arrows of the sky. Devoid of close vegetation, we are exposed to the elements; thankfully kind to us today. Visible even to dot-like humans far below who alert us silently, we wave in return.

The Lock of Witness

This account has made my spiritual journey as visible as the ancient narrowboat exhibited in the public waterway museum. Or, as prominent as a craft, sailing along the

Burnley Embankment. There's no hiding or deceiving. Visitors explore, test the comfort of the living area and examine the gaudy paintwork for symbolic commentary on the journeys it has sailed. The exhibited craft offers tourists a rich experience, meanings and interpretations long beyond its active usefulness as a vessel of transport.

God made it clear to me that my life-story was to be offered as an encouragement to those who struggle to believe that He will do what He has said. Not because He can't, but because we think He might not. Most of us have a significant battle with Him over this, especially those of us born in the Western world, influenced by scientific reason and the quest for rational explanation and evidence.

I think you may appreciate my honesty. There is no substitute for gutting it out. But in the morass of disappointment, delay and frustration, just a bit of mutual support, even if it comes from history, is a gift to each day. It's what I searched for - a genuine but critically appraising outside view that told me I was not going mad. That is why I believed I had to write to you, to encourage you that people still do crazy things with absolute conviction. People like Canon Andrew White, the Bishop of Iraq, who experienced the horrific persecution of the twenty-first century Christian church and out-stayed all reasonable risk to tell the tale and advocate for his church[1].

There will be a very public quest of all quests.

It is a quest for the prosperity of your soul. It was a public affair for me.

I remember how it was before the things I hoped for ever became apparent. When you have a kingdom leadership call upon your life, it is an absolute necessity to cultivate a vibrant and dynamic faith walk. It also feels to be an unmentionable deficiency to be weak in faith and trust. Where else can you go for help but to the feet of God? When He is silent? When the enemy of your soul rages from the split second of awakening or when the Father seems distant?

For me, the navigation of this quest took many years. I felt it acutely. During this time, I quit my professional nurse education career. I painfully adjusted focus on my unpaid pastoral role, leaving our household with only one part time meagre income. During this time, I also took up a clear need for personal counselling and, consequently, marriage guidance. I negotiated my children's teenage years and prayed for their struggle to transition through angst into the mature, gracious people they became.

Mine is only one of many unique stories providing certain hope that God is involved in the details and the crises, the transitions and eventual triumphs. If I had my time again, I would certainly have paid much more attention. I would have been truthful, brutally honest about the price of the dream I was chasing. My view now is that He didn't require me to pay such a cost. That cost has great value to Him - none of it is lost. However, it did not add the value it was meant to, right here and now.

For that I am sorry.

God told me to write this book as if it had already happened, unfolded and events transpired. So, from where I stand, it is yet to be seen. I had prepared to leave full time employment with no prospect of an income, as I naïvely claimed to a fellow pastor; *"I want to be one of those who have believed without seeing"*. Little did I imagine how seriously God would take that and what a tortuous journey I was embarking upon.

> *"He said, "Go to the Temple and take your stand. Tell the people everything there is to say about this Life."*
>
> (Acts 5:20 The Message)

And that is what I did!

I started to speak it, let it out, confessed and warred with it. I began to let *my life* as well as my words, *declare*. A disciplined mind, sober living and hope set on His grace and obedience became evident. This was the re-connection of the original call of an unschooled life with the incredible and unique destiny purposed before time began.

I recall that back in 1997, an international travelling prophetic minister visiting South Yorkshire, picked me out of the crowd where I was seated high in a church gallery[2]. She pronounced some breath-taking prophecy over my life. Including this,

"When I roar, who cannot but prophesy?"

This links with many Scriptures showing that God would have His way and that I could trust His word and flow with it and expect that it would be the primary and leading reality in my life.

When I stumbled across Acts 5:20, I knew that God was saying that I yet had to come to a place where I would stand, where I would declare the truth in a new capacity. It would be the whole doctrine of truth on a firm new footing. Peter and John were charged in these verses with the crime of preaching in the streets. They were sure that they would rather stand accused by the courts for having done so than by God for not speaking. They were charged with having flooded the city with their doctrine and despite all the risks of imprisonment, Peter and the apostles said, "We must obey God rather than men".

I too, felt this compulsion.

1 Corinthians 9:16 states *"I feel compelled of necessity to do it"*.

Despite nervousness about people's reactions, inability to follow through and serve God, I could do nothing else. And so, I came to be more scared of staying in secure work than I was of leaving the security of salary. I could not bear the thought of never knowing what might have happened if I had given it a go.

On the day I resolved to seek my release and give my notice to my boss, I experienced one of the busiest shifts of my nursing career. By mid-morning, I was still carrying the resignation letter that seemed to burn a hole in my pocket all that day. I'd tried frantically to call a mental health team for advice about an escapee hospice patient whom I had spent all morning trailing around the hospital grounds in the drizzling rain that November day in 2005.

My approach was that of Nehemiah. I had already taken a part-time reduction by leaving the teaching element of my role. Now, I returned to the "King" for a further granted favour. Throughout, I had my heart in my mouth because *this was it*. I might be released by Christmas. I asked for God to remember me for good and imprint me on His heart as Nehemiah had. My boss was gracious and receptive. I was spared any bad feelings and sensed a new future unfolding.

A 'New Thing' begins with declaration

First my husband and I discussed and decided. I then told my best friend and then my boss before the news went further afield to the church and my parents and then casual acquaintances.

God himself declares the future. In Isaiah 43, I see the Bible scholars must have struggled with their tenses as much I have done in this book.

"I have declared and saved, I have proclaimed, and there was no foreign god among you; therefore you are My witnesses," says the LORD, "that I am God. Indeed before the day was, I am He"

(Isaiah 43:12-13, NKJV)

Not long after leaving work, in early February 2006, this early teaching of mine, *As If*, was the focus of my attention. Less than three weeks since leaving employment I was already wrestling with issues of identity and acceptability to God, the lure of human works and efforts. As I read this earlier journal entry, I felt a firm nudge by God that this was the time to start writing again.

I had always considered that if I wrote the book *As If*, it would be because I had a platform and a voice that is valued as having "something credible to say". Here I was - still floundering. The book was shelved.

Instead I wrote about overcoming frustration[3].

I couldn't write about a great marriage, an overcoming faith or a family that prayed together and stayed together. I hadn't lived it and so I couldn't write it.

Then I realised - God valued me as having something to say NOW. And if He insisted on it now it had better be now. He wanted me to write this story called *As If* from the perspective of having arrived, having received the tangible blessing and fruit and growth. He wanted me to write it from the completion of the journey before I even got there.

He wanted me to stand *there* in advance, even if I had an imperfect gait and an ugly limp. In fact, only because I had an imperfect gait and an ugly limp did I need to stand in faith rather than ability.

There is a Scripture about the great spiritual battle we are engaged in to advance the Kingdom of God - often misquoted by leaving off the second part of the sentence.

They triumphed over him by the blood of the Lamb

(Revelation 12:11a, NIV)

Here it is in full.

They triumphed over him by the blood of the Lamb and by the word of their testimony; they did not love their lives so much as to shrink from death.

(Revelation 12:11, NIV)

Why did Jesus tell stories?

Why do we love stories?

They speak of a principle from a vulnerable place of example and authenticity, which is genuinely attractive and compelling. He wanted me to declare a new perspective of favour, fulfilment, testimony and glorification. I would write this story as if it had all unfolded, happened already and been completely and utterly fulfilled.

My declaration would become my testimony - and note that in this act of faith (to write), great boldness was endowed. So much so that I did not even shrink from death; the death of a vision, a mission or *even a purpose.*

I found that my only purpose is in sharing in His death.

This is how I found the courage to roar.

CHAPTER 15
WHEN I ROARED

Into the heart of Burnley, the heavily industrialised landscape now closes in again on us as the waterway cuts through the preserved cotton manufacturing "Weavers Triangle". We pass the glorified heritage of the carefully preserved spinning mills and weaving sheds, alongside nineteenth century worker's terraces. Their lives then were excruciatingly taxing. Generations of factory workers knew little other than simple sustenance and self-sufficiency. Long hours in noisy and dusty atmospheres took their toll upon respiratory health and hearing. Repetitive actions, repetitive shifts and repetitive seasons lulled whole communities into hypnotic passivity in the same way music, media and information overload did us, in the early twenty-first century.

I want to shout, "Wake up!", "Look up" and "Break out!" all at once. Can anyone even sense their confinement and congestion? For me it's painfully obvious as I slide by upon the inky waters toward another bend.

The eastern portal of Gannow Tunnel looms. We have determined to walk the half a kilometre tunnel. There is no towpath, no tugboat, simply our commitment to test our strength and knowledge, to walk through, in the traditional technique that will lead us through the dank and bat infested corridor to the western side. Shouting encouragements to each other that reverberate in the narrow clearance, my mate and I shuffle into place onto protruding planks at opposite points of extremity. Leaning only on the plank, perpendicular to the narrowboat's hull, we are eager to test our conviction that "we can do this".

The Lock of Boldness

The contemporary prophet's words spoken over me in 1997, *"when I roar, who cannot but prophesy?"* are from Amos 3:8, as a portent of God's judgement expressed through the shepherd prophet.

What is this connection between the lion and the prophet? Just as a lion cannot prevent its roar from rousing fear, neither can a prophet be restrained from declaring a prophetic word to the people.

Some of the Biblical prophets are recognised as melancholic; characters that did not necessarily see the fulfilment of their words, who may have struggled with fear, depression and insecurity, like Jeremiah and Elisha.

Like me. They were compelled to do it and could not be restrained from doing it. Whether anyone was listening or comprehending.

Like the legger's plank-lying, seemingly at cross purposes to the direction of narrowboat travel, their prophetic words and acts seemed incomprehensible to all that heard their warnings.

Tunnel walker

Around the time I was nearing completion of this book I received some quite shocking feedback from a platform conference keynote I had delivered a few weeks earlier. It seemed I had hit the mark with barely a handful of people. The others had struggled to comprehend my content and my vulnerability as anything other than anger and self- absorption.

This was extremely difficult and hurtful feedback to hear and I felt it as a direct attack upon my confidence and general call as a communicator. I was thrown into a slump of doubt about my capacity to deliver this message and a torrent of accusation from the enemy that my story is little more than narrow, brooding and narcissistic self-expression. No one would 'get it' and no one would even care to finish reading it, let alone be helped by it. Before long I had written my material off as depressing, incomprehensible and toxic.

No doubt there was room for improvement in my delivery; however, it seemed that the general message had been rejected out of hand. It was as if I was 'legging' a cumbersome vessel through an inhospitable tunnel. My roar had fallen on deaf ears.

As I came to the last weeks of this book writing journey, I stumbled across a clip of an interview with the main actor of *The Passion of Christ* (2004) directed by Mel Gibson[1]. I was spellbound by the testimony of Jim Caviezel[2], a Hollywood actor and committed Christian who played Jesus through the last twelve hours of his physical life on earth in the highest grossing 'R'-rated domestic film and the highest grossing non-English-language film of all time.

The humility of this interviewee was astonishing. He shared how he had committed himself to the preparation of this role with sincere dedication, even suffering a repeatedly

243

dislocated shoulder during the cross-lifting scenes, becoming seriously ill with pneumonia, accidentally subjected to a fourteen-inch laceration from the Roman lash and, being filmed on the cross during an actual thunderstorm.

Such was his identification with the suffering of Christ.

So, when Jim was diagnosed with a heart condition just prior to being 'crucified' it was reported to Mel Gibson *"He could die"*. However, Jim chose to risk his life by continuing the set believing that he must represent Christ to the best of his ability. (He required corrective open-heart surgery post-filming). Jim said,

"I'd become him"

"There was a conversation going on between me and God", he explained. He was ready to 'go home' as his actual death during filming could bring a harvest of souls through such a dramatic twist. Evidently, Jim was under a kind of parallel attack. As God asked him *"How far do you want to go with this?"* he tasted the cup of Jesus' own surrender and agreed with God to drain every drop of it.

His total identification with Christ was convicting. As an actor he had birthed this production in pain. There was the physical preparation of training and the consequences of injury, as well as the spiritual commitment to pray and fast, to meditate and stay in character.

The gravity of his words reminded me of the experience my old pastor Lilian once told of a time she had personally attended a meeting with Richard Wurmbrand[3]. This Romanian Christian minister who publically declared that Christianity and Communism were incompatible, was imprisoned and tortured for years before dedicating his life to advocacy for the persecuted church. Lil said of him *"he was too good for this world; it was like sitting at the feet of Christ"*.

The role-play had marked Jim with a similarly palpable authority, holiness and presence. It was as if Jesus himself was perched on the barstool being interviewed for this huge auditorium of church believers. And it was very uncomfortable and exposing to listen to Jim/Jesus. Even the interviewing host pastor appeared to become ashamed of his own jocularity as the interview proceeded and Jim broke into arresting Aramaic, Jesus' native language learned for the film.

Where are the tunnel walkers?

Why do I relate all this?

What was it that demanded such a commitment from Jim to be 'in role', even in the face of similar suffering as Jesus endured? Even through this testing 'tunnel' unto the point of death?

His perspective on life changed because of 'dying'. Now he had a 'roar' that stopped everyone in their tracks. Like C.S. Lewis' Aslan who believed there was a Deeper Magic beyond that which the White Witch was aware of, he submitted himself to the threat of a fatal execution. He was frustrated in order that he might experience and retrieve liberation for all.

"Death itself would start working backwards"[4].

This is better than life itself, this is resurrection.

> *I have been crucified with Christ and I no longer live, but Christ lives in me. The life I now live in the body, I live by faith in the Son of God*
>
> (Galatians 2:20, NIV)

Just like Paul, he might have added,

For I am already being poured out like a drink offering, and the time for my departure is near. I have fought the good fight, I have finished the race, I have kept the faith. Now there is in store for me the crown of righteousness, which the Lord, the righteous Judge, will award to me on that day—and not only to me, but also to all who have longed for his appearing.

(2 Timothy 4:6-8, NIV)

Like Jesus, Aslan, Paul and Jim we find courage at what looks like the very end of our life's navigation. We are simply at the point of departure and beginning, rather than our arrival and its ending.

It is as if this life is all just a rehearsal.

CHAPTER 16
AS IF

The view from the narrowboat

Having conquered the tunnel, we are relishing the open countryside once again. Changeable, mild gusts stir the rustling canal-side reeds. Bursts of sunshine spill onto the fields. Revealing a gossamer net of cobwebs, silver candy floss drapes the grassy banks. Yellow Iris and Meadowsweet fringe the red mud selvedge of the arable land. Jewel-like maiden-fly dart briskly, like a tailor's pins thrown into the midday haze. Water-boatmen skate and hesitate whilst moorhens scuttle crying into the overhang. Picnicking children share their crusts with the greedy mallard. One female is choking violently. Mottled light bounces off the inner arch of the approaching bridge, now grassed and redundant, a waving point for the party of cycling kids. Pooh sticks is a fruitless endeavour here as the water inches forward, merely glitters until the prow ruches the surface, sliding into the stone channel, scattering blocks of colour in its wake, confetti white, sunny yellow, scarlet and green on the water's surface.

The Lock of Assurance

When hope is disappointed, faith cannot be effective.

"But when desire is fulfilled, it is a tree of life"

(Proverbs 13:12)

Remember, that hope precedes faith and faith matures into deep trust, the fruit of that tree of life. I have learned there are two important requirements so that hope is not disappointed in its early fragility. These prevent hope from being deferred and the heart-sickness this causes.

First, you must stand (in hope) with expectation

You are living a prophetic life. Hope is still intangible. The power of the spoken word reinforces it by rousing you prophetically to see what cannot be seen in the natural realm.

So, what is prophecy?

Prophecy tells us *what* to hope for, because it does not originate in a man's will but God's speaking by the Holy Spirit.

It's not prediction. That only puts you in someone else's control or manipulation. Prophecy is truth, and it is the empowerment of God's timeless voice to you. It's simply God speaking to you. It's calling things that are not, as if they are and will be. It's the delivery of a God-communication, in His timing and with a right attitude. It is inspired revelation.

You take His word, in advance and live as if it were true. Like Isaiah who walked naked and barefoot for three years around Israel at God's command[1]. Like Jeremiah, whose message was scorned, you continue to warn and implore your contemporaries to believe. Like Job in the face of mass bereavement, financial ruin, broken health and utter contempt - despite your questions, implied shame, guilt and God's utter silence, you declare that you know that your Redeemer lives.

You must hope for the right things.

You do not hope with half-heartedness and certainly not in unbelief. Not if you want to stand 'as if' your hope will come true. Not if you want to live 'as if' you believe God's word.

Yes, hope is...

> "the glorious riches of this mystery, which is Christ in you, the hope of glory"

> (Colossians 1:27, NIV)

> "For what is our hope, our joy, or the crown in which we will glory in the presence of our Lord Jesus when he comes? Is it not you?"

> (1 Thessalonians 2:19, NIV)

Then, second, apply your faith to this hope.

Visualise standing at the finale—looking back on what lies ahead.

> "We have peace with God through our Lord Jesus Christ, through whom we have gained access by faith into this grace in which we now stand. And we rejoice in the hope of the glory of God. Not only so, but we also rejoice in our sufferings, because we know that suffering produces perseverance; perseverance, character; and

character, hope. And hope does not disappoint us, because God has poured out his love into our hearts by the Holy Spirit, whom he has given us."

(Rom 5:1-5, NIV)

You gain access by faith into this grace[2] in which you now stand.

See what is coming

The word *hazit (chazit)*[3] in Hebrew means 'to forecast' or to *'see what is to come'*. In addition, hazit also means 'frontline'. To stand on the frontline means to see what is to come. In fact, to have the courage to be on a frontline requires that one has already 'seen' a vision of a preferred future. Ironically, this 'seeing' allows far greater comfort with risk and commitment to cost. The Bible states that *without* a vision the people will perish[4], rather than because of one!

Yes, with a vision, despite great danger *with* conviction, one is safer than in comfort without vision.

And if I'm honest, I was up there on the frontline with a vision that didn't convince me to the core. Nor I was I convinced I could ever fulfil it.

This was very dangerous.

Because of this I was experiencing a kind of ministry 'shell shock'.

Warfare at the frontline

The frontline is a dangerous place where warring parties clash across a space or gap between two facing sides. It is the advancing edge of a kingdom that requires enormous courage and resolve for those who press forward into virgin or enemy territory. It is where the surrendered will to a higher cause touches the void of the unknown. All the while, one sees the risks of attaining to some preferred future, as a worthwhile sacrifice.

The root of this Hebrew word *chazit* is '*le chazot*'[5], to vision or see prophetically, to see what is not 'as if' it was. However, my compassionate heart, elaborate imaginative powers and overblown sense of responsibility had exercised a contaminating effect upon my eyes of faith. As I reached and strategised and travelled forward, delusions about the future grew like a gas-filled lump of dough doomed to collapse in on itself.

I was steering a fantasy. I had somehow deceived myself.

I can say that on the frontline, under extreme pressure and facing the void of extinction, one's mind can play tricks. Desperation, all too easily bursts out of relentless exposure. There are booby-traps one barely manages to keep avoiding.

Only the living word of direction and its deep heart assurance, will give you the resolve and focus to navigate such a course. Then and then only, may fantasy be steered into faith and destiny rise from delusion.

Emboldened by the Word of life

A word may come unconditionally. The Word (*logos*[6] in the Greek) is like a water well, a source of fresh water made available for access to us as a Bible to read. It is a reliable source of truth and life and principles for wholeness, perfect in its entirety. However, when you draw a bucketful of water from that well for a specific thirst in time and place, you may receive a conditional '*now*' word (In Greek this is called rhema[7]). It may be personal and directive but still relies on your application of belief and obedient embracing of the principles.

Take, for example, a woman who discovers that she is pregnant. *"I'm expecting!"* the mother may announce. Conception was hoped for within the legitimate covenant relationship of a loving commitment between two parents. She expected the child. Pregnancy is spoken of with excitement.

However, she might speak of it differently if the child is conceived under different circumstances. As the saying goes in the regions of Hull, *"She got caught!"*

Perhaps a teenager becomes pregnant or a mature woman has 'an accident' long after she has completed her family. Or, a victim of rape is impregnated. Then she talks of the event with a different tone.

Take Abraham and Sarah's story. Their ability to hold on to the promise of a child combining their own elderly DNA was circumvented when Abraham slept with his maidservant Hagar. Ishmael was conceived by his father's own efforts. Ishmael, as The Message Bible puts it, was the fruit of faithless connivance[8]. This first child was not ordained. Although God loved and blessed him in his own right, this child brought no fulfilment to the original promise.

You can deny it, doubt it or try to make it happen, but God just asks you to believe and declare it!

The Bible tells you that the spirit of Jesus (of testimony) is a prophecy that blesses those that take it to heart[9]. It also tells you that prophecy is for believers and not unbelievers[10]. So, ask your-self first, *"What do I hope for?"* and *"Am I approaching my sincere desire with belief?"*. Knowing that it is something God has told you to hope for, releases you to stand and declare in expectation.

Remember, viewing a desire *as if it* **has** happened *is faith* but saying to yourself or even God, *"Yeah, as if!"* is fantasy.

We are all faced with a choice of how to respond to the promises of God for our lives!

The Four 'If's

In Biblical Greek language, there are many subtle variations on any theme which add depth and accuracy to the meaning of the scriptures studied. When interpreters translate from the original into English, these nuances are lumped together and tidied up. So, we lose the original depth or even absolute meaning of a word like "love" or the simple word "if".

Yes, there is an "If-word" family.

I want to introduce you to the family of "Ifs"[11]. Just as there are different characters in any family, these are all very different even though they share the same name. In the same way, one faith could be many kinds of faith.

Sometimes you stray from a full understanding of the rich inheritance that is yours in Christ Jesus. For example, let's consider faith as interpreted by these four characters. You might recognise your kind of faith as characterised by one of these guys.

The If Family

- *Mr. If*

If - The Greek meaning of If is to say *If...and it isn't*

Mr. If is to **DENY your destiny and rather accept the tangible present and physical circumstances. The barrier to real faith here is physical fact.**

> **Mr If says:** *If I were you, I'd... (Of course, he is not you)*
> *If I win the lottery, I'll buy you all a holiday! (Oh really!)*
> *If I were you, I'd go for a home birth! (You're not me!)*
> *If I could believe (But I can't)*

This is the lowest faith form, it's fantasy, unreality.

This isn't faith—it's unbelief.
I don't want to do life **as if** I am Mr. If. He's driven by an over inflated self-importance and disregard of others. He is a very deceiving character and I advise you to keep him out of your world.

> *Your accuser is Moses, on whom your hopes are set. If you believed Moses, you would believe me, for he wrote about me. The hope is wrongly invested in Moses because they say they do believe in Him (in whom they do not believe!)*

> (John 5:45-46, NIV)

- **Now Meet Mrs. "If"**

If -The Greek meaning of this character is to say *If only...*

Mrs. If says *I wish...but...*

> If I could go to college,
> I might make something of my life
> If God healed me, my life would be better

Mrs. If's weakness is to DOUBT. She erects emotional barriers to what God has said. Hers is a faith based in need and discontent, even tinged with fear.

Do you want to live **as if** you are Mrs. If? She is a passive person who is driven by her feelings. Her view of need outweighs her view of God's ability to provide and this is paralysing. She hides in the arms of Jesus but flees from the devil who intimidates her and slashes her potential influence. She is a very unstable companion and I recommend that you give her a wide berth.

- ## Meet Miss "If"

If - The Greek meaning is to say *will it, or won't it? Or, it might, and it might not*

To be Miss If is to **IMPLEMENT, it is to be Miss Willpower Limited**

Miss If. says, *If I can…If he will*
    If I work harder, I might do well
    If I'm good, he'll love me
    If you hang in there, everything's gonna be all right!

Miss If demonstrates a wrong expression of faith too. This is based upon effort and activity, platitudes and even positive thinking. It will eventually fail because it is based on presumption. This If is motivated by doctrine and fear of failure to obey. It is a formula that will appear to work if you put it into operation with vigour. It is tinged with desperation and eventually falls apart if Miss If doesn't take some lessons from her brother. I don't want to live as if I regard life like Miss. If. She is a very driven person, exhausting, unnerving and uncomfortable to be around. She's forgotten that we are fighting a winning battle, a won battle.

Amazingly, God has limited himself to such an *"If and you might, and you might not"* type of uncertainty about you!

Will you or won't you come to Him?

He gives you this choice because God never messes with free will.

> *"If we confess our sins, he is faithful and just and will forgive us our sins and purify us from all unrighteousness"*

(1 John 1:9, NIV)

Wait, there's one more member of this family!

- **Meet Master If**

If - The Greek meaning is *If...and it is.*

To be MASTER If, is **to BELIEVE: to be spiritually alive and free.**

Master If says, *If you're their father, show them what you mean If it's Tuesday, it's market day*

This "if" is based on truth, fact, it's trustworthy and it's true. It's motivated by heart revelation. You need to get to know this If. He can teach you a lot. This member of the If family is also known as When, because, as far as he is concerned, what he believes has already happened.

This form of faith is confidence in the hoped for, certainty of what cannot be seen.

> *"If God is for us, who can be against us?"*

(Rom 8:31, NIV)

> *"She is clothed with strength and dignity; she can laugh at the days to come."*

(Proverbs 31:25, NIV)

Your spirit is invested with the capacity to view life from completion. It's your fickle and clamouring soul and physical body that convinces you that you are deluded, that these faith facts are out of reach. God wants you to dare to agree that what you see physically is less real than what He sees spiritually.

The great American preacher, TD Jakes said *"Dare to let go of the suffering, the worrying"*[12.] Yes, dare to deny your preoccupations. Life's trials are gifts to anoint us. What is meant to crush us can bless us. Believing the physical reality (Mr. If) and emotional pain (Mrs If) and relying on effort of will (Miss If) more than the future promise are the most dangerous temptations of all.

> *"I consider that our present sufferings are not worth comparing with the glory that will be revealed in us."*
>
> (Romans 8:18, NIV)

So, the antidote is to practise these promises **as if** they are and they will come naturally. Like Master If, deny the mental, physical, emotional and will power, asking God to,

> *"...give you the Spirit of wisdom and revelation, so that you may know him better. I pray also that the eyes of your heart may be enlightened in order that you may know the hope to which he has called you, the riches of his glorious inheritance in the saints, and his incomparably great power for us who believe."*
>
> (Ephesians 1:17-19, NIV)

UPRISING - BRIDGE

YOU MARVEL AT HIS PERFECT PLAN
YOU SAY, "IT IS FINISHED!"

By faith Jacob, when he was dying, blessed each of Joseph's sons, and worshipped as he leaned on the top of his staff.

(Hebrews. 11:21, NIV)

Jacob came home to his father Isaac in Mamre, near Kiriath Arba (that is, Hebron), where Abraham and Isaac had stayed. Isaac lived a hundred and eighty years. Then he breathed his last and died and was gathered to his people, old and full of years.

(Genesis. 35:27–29, NIV)

All the pages are numbered

"Where did you hide the bracelet?" asks Trea the next sunny morning as we breakfast in the morning garden pod.

Repeatedly, she fires her question as she stirs her chocolate porridge with ferocity. I'm wondering whether there's any merit in keeping my stash a secret. Anyway, there's something far more precious in the closet than even the gold bracelet. I consider revealing its whereabouts as I ponder another cup of caramel-coloured Yorkshire tea.

I've written a journal throughout my life. It ranges from an 8-year-old's laborious lists of meals eaten and TV programmes watched, interjected with the occasional teacher's criticism or schoolgirl secret. Right the way through, I documented all the familiar yet unique life transitions.

Once, I was convinced of a call to stop writing. Having read at 19 years of age, C S Lewis' testimonial *'Surprised by Joy'*[1] I had to agree with him that there could be a likely futility in diary writing. One day in eternity, I might well find there had been a difference of opinion between God and me. Everything I had recorded as of great importance might not reflect the moments and occasions He considered as of great significance! That's when I trusted Him to keep my accounts until a few years later I resumed the journaling habit with more reflection and prayer. Now it was of actual value to my spiritual and emotional health.

Now I face the dilemma of whether to disclose or to burn the piles of personal evidence. Of course, any value attributed to them would be in the eye of the beholder, so I am tempted to test Trea's reaction to the fact of their existence.

What have I got to hide?

I decide to give Trea a glimpse of my past, little knowing that in this moment she will grasp an inspiring vision of her future!

Hand in hand toward the basement closet we descend the new stairs. My heart is in my mouth and Trea's is bursting with joyful excitement. She discards her prized sketchbook full of elaborate *Specio* manifestations so she is free to handle the first bundle of diaries I extract.

I open the heavy lid to reveal piles and piles of colourful notebooks stacked in the antique chest. Hidden but not locked. I haven't answered the question *'Do I want anyone to read them?'* I suppose I feel less cautious as I approach the end of my life and accept that my life is one more imperfect example of humanity.

Surely the beauty of a story is in the vulnerability of its author? The Bible is not hesitant in painting the lives of its imperfect characters with no attempt to tidy up their faults.

"Did you write ALL these with a pen?" she marvels.

"Actually, the first few are written in pencil" I explain. *"We weren't allowed to use fountain pens until we were ten years old as we got in such a mess with the ink. We didn't have touchscreens or dicta-docs then"*.

She turns the pages in awe, squealing with delight at the odd little cartoon of a horse or teacher caricature. I myself am struck by the awkward naivety in one volume, the self-absorption of another and the dark confusion of many more. Phew, what a trial, and somehow, I think I have made sense of most of it.

The singer-songwriter, 'Sting' once reflected upon life's various chapters in *'The Book of my Life[2]'*,

"The end is a mystery no one can read - in the book of my life"

Isn't that what we think? And yet it needn't be a mystery. Life isn't a random or fated script. The pages are numbered. The bridges and locks are all numbered. And though we can never know life's factual detail in advance, we *can* trust the intention before the end of our days, even if we never understand it.

Nor is God a chapter as Sting suggested, He is the Beginning and the End!

Perhaps details such as the ones I have recorded all my life are temporarily fascinating. However, the real value of life, its outcome or product is a life lived consciously and humbly, with teach-ability. These are principles that work in advance when you seize and operate them *as if* they will work.

Trea has grasped this.

She can see that her life will look like this too one day, finished and accounted for. All the transitions of her growth are written *for her*. They will be written *by her* and will be open to scrutiny and enjoyment *by others*. As an open book, she will influence, live well and make His plans and purposes tangible once again,

On earth, as it is in heaven.

CHAPTER 17
THE LAST WORD

Weary from the seventy-metre descent of Wigan's twenty-one locks, we nevertheless agree that this was preferable to the challenges of ascent.

As a pleasurable finale, we turn into the Leigh branch of our journey, through Poolstock and onto the Wigan Flashes. Exploring this section of the Leeds-Liverpool canal we are brought out into acres of reclaimed colliery wasteland, now rich in wildlife and a magnet for nature lovers.

Rippling reeds blur the poorly defined canal's edge, daubed with banks of common spotted orchid and a haze of cow-parsley. The passing boat pushes the reed fronds into a gently bobbing dance, alarming an offended Great Crested Grebe from its siesta.

It is hard to believe how heavily polluted and industrialised this flatland once was. We catch one another's eyes in awestruck appreciation of the power of nature in reclaiming her ownership once more.

More than I could ever have possibly dared to dream or imagine

It is written,

> "I believed; therefore I have spoken."
> With that same spirit of faith we also believe and
> therefore speak"

(2 Corinthians 4:13, NIV)

I stand totally amazed at the favour and goodness of God over my life as it nears completion. I have been favoured with the indescribable honour of His rich presence and leading, blessing and influence, timing, opportunity and multiplication. This has been far more than I could ever have possibly dared to dream or imagine. Most generously, He has reimbursed and surpassed even the impossible toil and diminishment of the frustration years.

For God to have chosen such a driven, perfectionist, melancholic and self-conscious introvert is ridiculous. I was covertly prepared by the Spirit for a rude introduction to ministry and leadership. I defied all external odds and opposition, prolonged obscurity, battles with disappointment, inner defeat, divorce and depression.

First, I was passively aware of oppression, then earnestly responsive to resistance and finally aggressively battled all threats and intimidation, division and fear. Only God could have put the conviction in me to re-double as He did. Only He could have protected me from the finality of despair, the bad press, persecution and financial hardship that patterned my life.

He wonderfully drew my second-hand-picked husband and me into the same sphere so that we would miraculously find each other. (We always joked about the fact that I didn't know which it was, that he was the second, second-hand, or hand-picked.) He was certainly not my second *hand-picked* husband.

My first choice had been entirely my own undoing.

For the many years of re-orientation between my first and second marriages, I had been clear about one thing. I could not do life alone and I needed the power of partnership to go forward.

I knew this because I had tired of trying to do it all however valid the goal.

'Without a vision the people perish', said God[1].
'Without a plan the vision will perish', said Paul Scanlon[2].

"Without a vision, the people perish but without a plan the vision perishes".

'But I have a plan!' I had exclaimed bitterly (it was a really *thick* one).

Yes, I had got myself a plan, but it turned out to be a scam.

So I say,

"Perish my plan! Without God, the vision is a scam"

Maybe the plan was off-centre. However, it was the detail I had drowned in. There was housekeeping, networking, failed bids for elusive funding opportunities. Despite enthusing about marketing, dreaming up enterprise and social action projects and being noticed in the voluntary and community sector, the plan didn't materialise. Despite promoting friendship and street evangelism, sowing generous gifts and hearing from the best world class leaders on a regular basis, I couldn't *'convert'* leads, to use a business term.

Despite aiming for excellence in creating a platform for the ministry of the Word on a Sunday, this was often for a handful of people.

The team elevated principles, strong values, relationship, and integrity added to those of fellowship, servant-hood and generosity.

People did not come to any of those things.

We probably empowered people before their time. We taught our brains out. Often I spoke words prophetically. But gifted and even anointed words flowed through me that still hadn't bedded in me. They flowed through me but they weren't coloured by me. Once I was touched by the void within me, terrified by the emptiness and inadequacy, then I knew I was a hair's breadth between becoming an abject failure or a trophy of grace.

My husband and I had soul searched and prayed, we invested in other ministries and sat under the influence of great men and women of God on the international stage who themselves have gone down in history as world changers. A respected church leader seeing the strain showing on our faces, threw us a life line as he said to us one day,

"You two are more important than the church".

But my incomprehension at the time meant this caution was unheeded.

I knew that I had to put myself into a risky position where I could desperately seek effective faith.

Did I have such faith? I didn't know it would be the right degree of faith I would find to draw from. Instead, we drew on the re-mortgage equity release, the endowment policy and the modest life insurance plan.

I knew God was able…. I still had difficulty knowing whether He was willing.

At that point, my faith was that I would develop the required degree of faith. I certainly knew that I needed more of it, but beyond that need for more faith, God knew I needed to find Him - My Father. Yes I had a faulty image of God as a distant and coolly observant God. My extreme vulnerability put me on a collision course with a real communicative, doting, passionate intimate God.

Like me, many probably hang far too long on the lifeline of their own ability. God will even cut it and allow your expectations to come crashing down with you. It seems that everything you touch turns to ashes. This is humiliating and devastating to your confidence. You face silence, separation, rejection and death in the face. God allows this for a season. Eventually you stop, frustrated. The word you held out in appeal and genuine conviction, fails to lift and convict and implement change as you believed it was sent to do.

You are broken.

All your best efforts served what God alone can do.

Though they are fundamental to what you do, they will never bring about what only God can do… and that is to fill you, me, the precious Body of Christ, your city, the humbled nation Great Britain once again. Yes, the whole earth will be filled with the glory of God as the waters cover the seas.

How can that be?

It will be completely, invasively, heavily, and mysteriously. Beyond the reaches of our knowledge and understanding!

Now **that is a God-breathed vision AND implementation strategy.**

The imagination bursts from such an image and activity. *Then* you start to have something to celebrate.

And so, God unfolded the message 'As If' over my life, as a *declaration* of His goodness and power, to elevate ordinary, insecure, even unhappy and obscure people far beyond their wildest dreams. The delay and obstruction that littered my early ministry was heaven consented for my own benefit and growth, to refine a holy and consuming desire for Him that would anoint and inflame my message. That message, the message of my life, recorded here, has been battled out for you. That treasure found in the darkness, was for you!

Yes, the message that I have declared these years, is my life. The stand I declare from, is my life. Not the lucky break, the public platform or the good word put in for me. Nor even the sheer hard work of making things happen. *Your* life itself is also your platform. The Living Word can only speak and rouse and inspire others through lives He has taken and shaken experientially.

God says that your life is placed here and now with a unique arrangement of gift, call and style, through the craft of your personality, to deliver genius, influence and impact as if God Himself depended on it.

Because He really, really does.

I am thrilled, full of joy to testify that I finally believed! This is my greatest attainment and the one I have needed the most divine patience and assistance with. The hand of God was teaching me to judge myself soberly and to mistrust myself and my personal abilities and strengths. The irony of this conclusion is that as a broken person, I now had to assess whether mine was a valuable story worthy to be told.

Moreover, I was being asked to write it whilst only just developing this long sought-after foresight gift of faith, called "As If hindsight". Even as I was still emerging, I wrote as if I could see back from where I was going to review everything as an elderly woman who had run her race (or navigated her cruise). This is the same perspective God has of us, long before we deserve it.

He will,

> "Strengthen (complete, perfect) and make you what you ought to be and equip you with everything good that you may carry out His will; [while He Himself] works in you and accomplishes that which is pleasing in His sight, through Jesus Christ (the Messiah); to Whom be the glory forever and ever (to the ages of the ages) Amen (so be it)"

(Hebrews 13:21)

God gives a down-payment of faith as an advance deposit from this place on the horizon of our dreams. Looking back from it, as if I were already there I could see light streaking across all my days. I wrote it as if everything had already taken place, everything that God had said would happen. Even when it was still no more tangible than nearly twenty years earlier as I had started to write it.

The act of writing was a symbolic act of faith in the value of the story, of the book, of the market for it and preparation for the ministry of declaration on the stand that God was giving me. This stand rests upon the word, even amongst the circumstances still prevailing against me. It is a stand against the emotions that still regularly overwhelm me and through the myriad of thoughts that still intimidate me.

Navigating its way out of fantasy and delusion, wishful thinking and heedless presumption, the narrowboat of salvation carries you and me into the destiny of God's heart of love if we choose to travel in it.

Through escalating flights of testing we will arrive there.

Now, see *your* life also, as a compelling example of a worthwhile route. Prove yourself to be a convincing declaration of all your future certainties in and through it - though they cannot yet be seen.

This is your meandering and timeless, purposeful story of faith.

"*Earnestly remember the former things, [which I did] of old; for I am God, and there is no one else; I am God, and there is none like me, Declaring the end and the result from the beginning, and from ancient times the things that are not yet done, saying My counsel shall stand, and I will do all my pleasure and purpose*"

Isaiah 46:9-10

ACKNOWLEDGEMENTS

Sincere thanks to those of my Author Academy Elite peers who have taken the trouble to advise on my style and form. Stuart Lamont, thank you for responding to a request for beta readers. To writer Linda Zupancic and reader Amy Weise, I am grateful for your invaluable feedback upon a sample of my manuscript.

Thank you, Mary Chambers for your grammatical eagle eye and my dearest friend Julie, for believing in this message for so many years. You have continued to encourage me to write even when I was overwhelmed with life's challenges and the need to survive a season of pain. You provided a space to think and write and celebrated with me, the launch of my preceding title. That released the flow for this much slower creation.

To Kary Oberbrunner, entrepreneur, friend and author coach - when we met at a landmark conference in 2011, you sensed in me a fellow need to express my story. You re-ignited my desire to write when I told you about my half-written manuscript and inspired me with a copy of your signature story *Your Secret Name*. Thank you for steering me in this adventure and helping me to recognise the truth that I am an author!

Thank-you for buying AS IF!

Director, Lisa Miara
Springs of Hope Foundation

Ten percent of the royalties of the sales of As If will be donated to the precious work of Springs of Hope Foundation. Visit the stories here - springsofhope.foundation

This incredible NGO relies on acts of kindness and generosity from people like yourself whose hearts ache and whose conscience is stirred over the amazing, noble people, war refugees, Yezidis and other minority groups struggling to survive in Northern Iraq (post genocide) which the world continuously chooses to ignore. Such acts of giving never die. They enable us to remain with boots on the ground, breathing life into new acts of kindness in this hard region. We are inviting you to join our Culture of Giving. A tangible expression of your love and care that will be passed on to others in your name.

ABOUT THE AUTHOR

GILL BENTHAM is an author. Her sincere passion is to help people - *each of us one of seven billion geniuses* - get to know, love and liberate their inner genius. As a writer, content creator and insight coach, Gill is the indelible marker of individuals' life scripts. She helps them remember, recover and rewrite their trapped potential or tangled dreams. Then, they in turn leave a vital, permanent mark in their world.

A protracted season of hardship, failure and personal disappointments, forged a deep frustration in her heart that played havoc with her personal aspirations and expectations. Utilising a lifelong habit of self-discovery through journaling and intimacy with God, a powerful message of disentanglement and re-cycling emerged.

Her medium is her pen (or keyboard).

Her story is to encourage the opportunity and capacity for others to find their font and tell *their* story!

Whatever the medium by which their life speaks, finding THEIR powerful story is her quest.

Gill aims to make sense of the unintelligible;
rendering it indelible!

Her Amazon Profile https://www.amazon.com/-/e/B00IKTF26A

She lives in northern England with her second husband and has two adult children from her first marriage.

ABOUT THE FLOW OF FRUITION

Principles for growth, maturity, belonging and effectiveness in one's life, family, community and organisation are essential in life. Never quite finding fulfilment or the right timing in her early adulthood, Gill lost heart. She took a few years to re-align and understand what her own unique contribution could be. Not only as a single mother after 17 years of marriage, but with a disrupted career and reputation.

A learner and teacher at heart, Gill found herself disorientated in a very busy and confusing online market for self-development and commentary. She submitted to a process of refining and maturing, during a definite season of obscurity. And started to laugh at herself. Now she presents a message, the message of her life. Could there be a pattern in yours too?

Gill hosts learning modules in her 'Flow of Fruition' school through gillbentham.com where subscribers and students can access exciting growth principles' and wisdom for life material. This content is for personal, communal or corporate growth. If established in sequence and re-cycled throughout every new season of life or cycle of change, these time honoured principles will strengthen your capacity to work, wait, expect, hope and believe with absolute conviction for your ultimate fulfilment to come.

The secret is to expect the right fruit at the right stage of the cycle.

Connect at Teachable.com for my Flow of Fruition modules

Origin

Position

Function

Stature

Attraction

ABOUT THE INDELIBLE TRIBE

Gill wrote two books whilst surviving a tricky divorce, deepening debt and three redundancies. She brings a unique sense of calm, connection and deep value of the client, their back story and their ability to achieve. Not despite their traumas but because of them!

Because of this, she formed a tribe! We are called The Indelibles. If you meet us, you won't forget the mark we make upon you. Gill restores a sense of flourishing in life by facilitating provocative and colourful learning experiences face to face and online. These are set in a rich and fertile environment of self-growth.

The tribe gravitating toward this community feel secure, inspired and excited to exercise courage and creativity with their ideas. And soon they believe they can!

Are you an undiscovered or unfulfilled genius-in-waiting? Clients may request an invitation to the Indelible Tribe here:

facebook.com/gilldeclares/

Your Next Steps with 'As If'

How You Can Continue Steering Your Life Without Strife,
By Navigating Away from Fantasy toward Faith
And Rising above Delusion into Destiny

 **'As If' virtual 'Boat Trip'
- Free Masterclass**

 **'As If' virtual Navigation
- Cruise Module**

 **Downloadable 'As If'
Navigation Guide –
Complementary Learning
Journal**

All links at gillbentham.com/asif

Also, by Gill Bentham - Disentangling Genius

Disentangling Genius

This is a thrilling, adventurous treatment of frustration, an all too familiar waste of human potential. As a self-help guide, it is refreshingly honest, engaging and truly imaginative. She treats the subtle and deceitful sapping of personal genius with a novel approach. Exposure of our sabotaged uniqueness is a vital subject in a world of confusion about identity and purpose.

The author uses philosophical comment, humour and questions. She provokes opportunities for reflection and self-awareness. Through the metaphor of tangled wool and all its unused potential, she weaves into her journey, a series of fantasy, historical and contemporary genius characters who have demonstrated how to become untangled.

Colourful in imagery, richly inspiring and entirely practical in approach this is a stirring and surprising warning alert for readers who doubt their capacity to overcome unrelenting resistance in fulfilling their desires.

Associated content found at: gillbentham.com

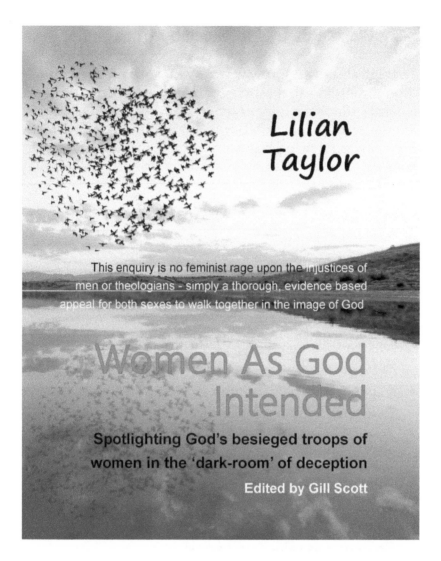

Lilian
Taylor

This enquiry is no feminist rage upon the injustices of
men or theologians - simply a thorough, evidence based
appeal for both sexes to walk together in the image of God

Women As God
Intended

Spotlighting God's besieged troops of
women in the 'dark-room' of deception

Edited by Gill Scott

Lilian Taylor's lifelong desire for this message to be published
was fulfilled by her editor, protégé and friend, Gill Scott
after Lilian's death in 2014.

Associated content found here: gillbentham.com

Women as God Intended by Lilian Taylor

There's already a growing conviction among Christian thought-leaders that women and men are equally essential in God's unfolding plan. A conspiracy was seeded in time immemorial by one who bitterly hates us - male or female. Enmity was released between woman and Satan. 'Women as God Intended' is a personal reflection and public inquiry into the fallout of this fatal blow.

In these pages you will

- Discover the truth - women were always central to the sweeping plan of God through eternity.

- Visit the story of every prominent woman in the Bible.

- Uncover the damage of tradition, religion or clumsily applied theology to Everywoman's unique voice.

- Expose strategic sabotage against women by the gates of Hell, to weaken God's plan of salvation for all.

- Realise this plot significantly impairs the mission of the Church and her revealing to the world.

- Celebrate the restoration of the Body of Christ today of Everywoman's part in the complementary power and partnership of man and woman.

- Be united as valued and equal.

All royalties are donated to the Hull Women's Refuge, Charity no 1160440

Your Bracelet Hunt Challenge

Within the text of *"As If"* I refer to the bracelet my elderly mother-in-law gave me to hand on to my baby daughter upon Esme's coming of age.

Esme often asked excitedly about when she could see it and it was a great day on the 2nd, October 2012 when Esme received her carefully wrapped gift, long after Roopea's death. To my dismay, last summer, Esme sheepishly told me that the ring had been snatched from her wrist on an evening out, in May 2018. This was a blow to the family heritage and a disruption to my anticipated tale of it becoming a family heirloom.

One thing this book hadn't anticipated to the degree it should have (about Great-Grandmother Gill's contemporary world) was the power and impact of social media. I'd love to harness that power now, in asking my readership to go on a quest to find Trea's rightful legacy. I wish to offer readers and listeners an exciting challenge of investigation for our precious, missing piece of jewellery.

What can you do to help in this endeavour?

I believe that one of you (or someone aware through you) will be able to report it has been found! Through the power of social media and our collective desire to receive Trea's bracelet back into its family ownership, we will find it again. Share through your social media channels and ask for everyone to be vigilant.

If you are the first person whose alert to me leads to its recovery, you will inherit a similar piece tailored to your family characteristics or symbolism.

Please find and share the photograph
and description below
or on this link.

facebook.com/gilldeclares/

Table of Pictures, Photographs and Diagrams

NOTES

Introduction

1. Gill Scott, *Disentangling Genius* (Author Academy Elite, 2014)
2. Bette Midler, "From a Distance", accessed 1st October 2017 https://youtu.be/EC3FW_RU-GI
3. Jeremiah 30:21 (TLB)
4. Watchman Nee, *Sit Walk Stand* (CLC Ministries, 2009)

Ch 1

1. Gill Scott, *She Who Dares* (Unpublished)
2. Ephesians 1:17-18
3. Watchman Nee, Unsourced

Ch 2

1. Acts 13:22
2. Robert Hotchkin, "Women on The Frontlines" Conference (Torquay: XP Ministries with Patricia King, 2016)
3. John 3:16

Ch 3

1. Mimi Leder, *Pay It Forward*, Nevada, USA, Warner Brothers, 2000.
2. Watchman Nee, *The Latent Power of the Soul* (Christian Fellowship Publisher, 1972)
3. Kris Valloton, *Fashioned to Reign* (Minnesota: Chosen Books, 2013)
4. Tests such as Myers-Briggs Type Indicator, DISC, StrengthsFinder 2.0, Belbin or Enneagram

Ch 5

1. Isaiah 50:7
2. Andrew Lloyd-Webber, Joseph "Will any dream do?"
3. http://www.droitwichcanals.co.uk/page24.html accessed 16th October, 2017.
4. Matthew 7:6
5. Paul Scanlon, https://www.lifechurchhome.com/ accessed 2nd October, 2017
6. Will worship, https://www.christiancourier.com/articles/1544-pauls-condemnation-of-will-worship, accessed 12th October 2017
7. Bobbie Houston "Colour Conference" (Wembley Arena, London, 2016)

Ch 6

1. 2 Thessalonians 2:1
2. Acts 1:10-11
3. Bill Hybels, *Courageous Leadership*. (Zondervan, 2002)
4. Pocket Oxford Dictionary
5. Genesis 1:28
6. Romans 5:12
7. Philippians 4: 19

8. Genesis 32:30
9. 1 Corinthians 1:30
10. Hebrews 11
11. http://edition.cnn.com/2001/US/09/15/bush.radio.transcript/, accessed 10th October 2017
12. John 24: 28
13. John 6: 25-29

Ch 7

1. Hebrews 9-11
2. 1 Samuel 2:8
3. Joe Simpson, *Touching the Void* (DirectAuthors.com Ltd, 1988)
4. Watchman Nee, *Secrets to Spiritual Power: From the writings of Watchman Nee*, compiled by Sentinel Kulp (Sunneytown PA: Whitaker House,1999), 43.
5. Gill Scott, *Disentangling Genius* (Author Academy Elite, 2014)
6. Michael Mann, *The Last of the Mohicans*, Colorado (USA), 20th Century Fox, 1992.

Ch 9

1. Delerious? *Stare the monster down,* Kingdom of Comfort (CD, 2008)
2. John 13:34-36
3. John 14:6

Ch 10

1. Bill Hybels, *Holy Discontent* (Zondervan, 2007)
2. Gill Scott, *Journal.* (Unpublished, 24th January 2007)

Ch 11

1. Jehovah-Jireh International, 14th October, 2017
2. David enquires of the Lord, 1 Samuel 30:8.
3. Pete Seeger, *Where have all the flowers gone? Sing Out! Magazine, 1955.*
4. Hurricane Katrina, https://en.wikipedia.orgwiki/Hurricane_Katrina, accessed 24th January, 2019.
5. Boscastle, UK, https://www.metoffice.gov.uk/learning/learn-about-the-weather/weather-phenomena/case-studies/boscastle, accessed 14th October, 2017
6. Toll Bar UK, http://www.doncasterfreepress.co.uk/news/how-the-ea-beck-flooded-toll-bar-1-508192, accessed 14th October, 2017.
7. Matthew Henry on Joshua 3:14-17, http://bit.ly/2ydn9Yt, accessed 14th October, 2017

Ch 12

1. Gill Scott, *Journal* (Unpublished, Circa.1999)
2. Paul Scanlon, https://paulscanlon.com/about/, accessed 2nd October 2017

Ch 13

1. Marva, J. Dawn, *The Sense of the Call* (William B. Eerdmans Publishing: Cambridge, 2006) 36.

Legacy, the Reclaimed Promise

1. Kary Oberbrunner, *Your Secret Name* (Zondervan: Michigan, 2010)

Ch 14

1. Canon Andrew White, https://en.wikipedia.org/wiki/Andrew_White_(priest), accessed 10th October 2017
2. Sharon Stone, International Speaker (Wakefield New Life Christian Centre, UK, March 1998)
3. Gill Scott, *Disentangling Genius* (Author Academy Elite, 2014)

Ch 15

1. Mel Gibson, *The Passion of Christ,* http://www.imdb.com/title/tt0335345/, accessed 20th September 2017
2. Jim Caviezel, https://youtu.be/0Ejaw0F8-sY, accessed 20th September 2017.
3. Richard Wurmbrand, *Tortured for Christ,* https://en.wikipedia.org/wiki/Richard_Wurmbrand, accessed 20th September 2017
4. C. S. Lewis, *The Lion, the Witch and the Wardrobe* (Harper Collins, 2009)

Ch 16

1. Isaiah 20:2-3.
2. Joyce Meyer, *If not for the Grace of God* (Faithwords, 2002)
3. Hebrew, chazit/hazit
4. Proverbs 29:18
5. Hebrew, le chazot
6. Logos, Greek, https://en.wikipedia.org/wiki/Logos_(Christianity), accessed 21st September 2017
7. Rhema, Greek, *Vine's expository Dictionary of New Testament Words* (Marshall Pickering Communications, 1952)
8. Galatians 4:21. The Message Bible.
9. Revelation 1:3
10. 1 Corinthians 14:22

11. If, http://www.biblefood.com/condsent2.html, accessed 20th September 2017
12. TD Jakes, International Speaker (Mega Fest, 2005)

All the pages are numbered

1. C S Lewis' testimonial *'Surprised by Joy'* (Collins, 2012)
2. Sting, *'The Book of My Life'* with lyrics, https://youtu.be/BXvejBDkdu8, accessed 2nd October 2107

Ch 17

1. People perish, Proverbs 29:18
2. Paul Scanlon, https://paulscanlon.com/about/, accessed 2nd October 2017.

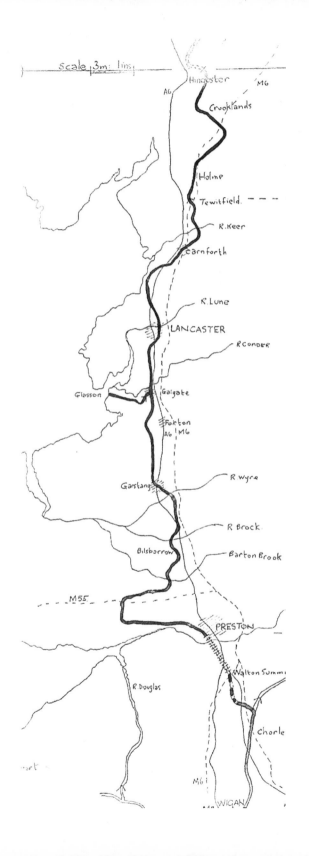

Scale 3m : 1ins

Hincaster
M6
A6
Crooklands

Holme
Tewitfield.
R. Keer
Carnforth

R. Lune
LANCASTER
R CONDER

Glasson
Galgate

Foxton
A6 M6

R Wyre

Garstang

R Brock.
Bilsborrow
Barton Brook

M55

PRESTON
Walton Summit
R. Douglas
Chorle

M6
WIGAN

Lightning Source UK Ltd.
Milton Keynes UK
UKHW011609080519
342322UK00001B/134/P